Best Easy Day Hikes
Santa Fe

Help Us Keep This Guide Up to Date

Every effort has been made by the authors and editors to make this guide as accurate and useful as possible. However, many things can change after a guide is published—trails are rerouted, regulations change, facilities come under new management, and so forth.

We welcome your comments concerning your experiences with this guide and how you feel it could be improved and kept up to date. While we may not be able to respond to all comments and suggestions, we'll take them to heart, and we'll also make certain to share them with the author. Please send your comments and suggestions to the following address:

FalconGuides
Reader Response/Editorial Department
246 Goose Lane
Guilford, CT 06437

Or you may e-mail us at:
editorial@falcon.com

Thanks for your input, and happy trails!

Best Easy Day Hikes Series

Best Easy Day Hikes Santa Fe

Third Edition

Linda Regnier and Hope Di Paolo

FALCONGUIDES

GUILFORD, CONNECTICUT
HELENA, MONTANA

FALCONGUIDES®

An imprint of Rowman & Littlefield

Falcon and FalconGuides are registered trademarks and Make Adventure Your Story is a trademark of Rowman & Littlefield.

Distributed by NATIONAL BOOK NETWORK

Copyright © 2006, 2016 by Rowman & Littlefield
Published in 1999 by Falcon Publishing, Inc.

Maps: Melissa Baker © Rowman & Littlefield

British Library Cataloguing-in-Publication Information available

The Library of Congress has cataloged a previous edition as follows:
Regnier, Linda.
Best easy day hikes Santa Fe | Linda and Katie Regnier
Helena, MT : Falcon Pub., c1999.
LCCN 99029378 | ISBN 1560447001 (pbk.)
LCSH : Hiking—New Mexico—Santa Fe Region—Guidebooks.
    Santa Fe Region (N.M.)—Guidebooks.
LCC GV199.42.N62 S277 1999 | DDC 917.89/5604/53 record available at https://lccn.loc.gov/99029378

ISBN 978-1-4930-1784-3 (paperback)
ISBN 978-1-4930-1785-0 (e-book)

∞™ The paper used in this publication meets the minimum requirements of American National Standard for Information Sciences—Permanence of Paper for Printed Library Materials, ANSI/NISO Z39.48-1992.

Contents

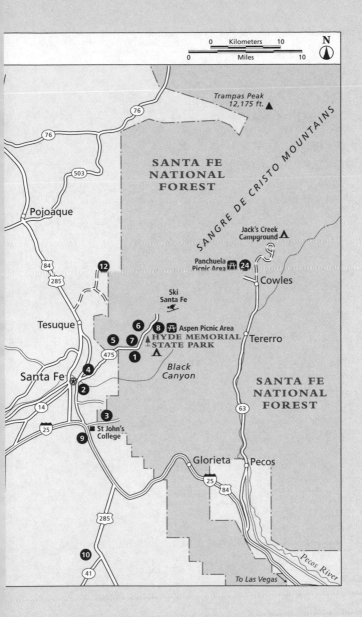

Acknowledgments

This third edition would not exist were it not for Jim Regnier. Linda was unable to hike due to a foot injury, so it fell to Hope and Jim to carry on. Very alike in many ways, they put their heads down, hiked uphill and down, and broke all kinds of speed records. It was difficult, therefore, to calculate approximate hiking times; we did the best guesstimate. We will happily share all royalties with Jim, husband and grandfather.

Our hike to the Pecos Wilderness was especially eventful, as we met Libby Mims and her mother, Jean Jorgenson, both with long histories in the Pecos, and Alice McSweeney, proprietor of Los Pinos Ranch, located just before Panchuela picnic ground at the Cave Creek Trailhead. We received a personal tour of this historic ranch, and we encourage you to visit www.lospinosranch.com for further information.

Our thanks to William Tefft, manager, New Mexico Public Lands Information Center in Santa Fe; Dr. Glenda King of Santa Fe Foot and Ankle Institute, who recommended a great new hike; Gregg Ohlsen of Travel Bug in Santa Fe; and, last but not least, Jandy Cox of Rocky Mountain Outfitters in Kalispell, Montana, who provided us his technical expertise.

Ranking the Hikes

Easiest → More Challenging

Introduction

> Climb the mountains and get their good
> tidings. Nature's peace will flow into you
> as sunshine flows into trees. The winds
> will blow their own freshness into you,
> and the storms their energy, while cares
> will drop away from you like the leaves of
> autumn.
>
> —John Muir

The hope for this third edition of *Best Easy Day Hikes Santa Fe* is to allow hikers of all levels of ability and time constraint to enjoy the same pleasures that John Muir found in nature. In an effort to ensure all hikes truly fall under the category of "best easy," all routes are less than 6 miles. The hikes cover a variety of areas and terrains in northern New Mexico, but all are within a short drive from the center of Santa Fe. This book aims to provide exposure to the multitude of experiences that hiking in and near Santa Fe can provide.

Simultaneously, we hope the guide encourages hikers to go beyond the routes we have included and to explore further the regions described. By no means a complete listing of the best easy day hikes, *Best Easy Day Hikes Santa Fe* begs the reader to go beyond the pages of this book and into the good tidings Santa Fe hiking has to offer.

The Santa Fe area of northern New Mexico offers a diverse collection of trails through mountains, valleys, canyons, high desert terrain, and a multitude of ecosystems. It is rare to find yourself among such a variety of hikes while maintaining such logistical convenience. All routes featured in this book are easily accessible and within a ninety-minute drive of the Santa Fe plaza.

Adding to the appeal of Santa Fe hiking, the climate of northern New Mexico extends an opportunity for hiking at any time of year, through all four seasons. Most trails in this edition are maintained and in good condition 365 days a year. Moderate winters allow for hiking in the valley and much of the high desert regions. Summer temperatures are especially conducive to mountain hiking, which provides lower ambient temperatures and cool breezes. Freezing temperatures are rare in the Santa Fe area, except in the mountains on occasion. What's more, a pleasant 283 days of sun each year beg hikers to hit the trails no matter the season.

The hikes offered in this edition have been quite deliberately chosen for their accessibility, distance, and significance. Most hikes are close to attractions of cultural, archaeological, geological, and historical importance. Whether it is an afternoon hike amid the remarkable geological formations of Kasha-Katuwe Tent Rocks National Monument or a morning excursion through the unexcavated Ancestral Pueblo village of Tsankawi, Santa Fe-area day hiking does not disappoint.

Zero Impact Hiking

A wilderness can accommodate plenty of human use as long as everybody treats it with respect. But a few thoughtless or uninformed visitors can ruin it for everyone who follows. And the need for good manners applies to all wilderness visitors, not just backpackers. Day hikers should also adhere strictly to the Leave No Trace principles. Visit LNT.org for more details and suggestions.

Leave No Trace Principles

- Plan ahead and Prepare
- Travel and Camp on Durable Surfaces
- Dispose of Waste Properly
- Leave What You Find
- Minimize Campfire Impacts
- Respect Wildlife
- Be Considerate of Other Visitors

Most of us know better than to litter—in or out of the wilderness. Even the tiniest scrap of paper left along the trail or at a campsite detracts from the pristine character of the landscape. This means that you should pack out everything, even biodegradable items such as orange peels, which can take years to decompose. It's also a good idea to pick up any trash that less considerate hikers have left behind.

To avoid damaging the trailside soil and plants, stay on the main path. Avoid cutting switchbacks and venturing onto fragile vegetation. When taking a rest stop, select a durable surface like a bare log, a rock, or a sandy beach.

When nature calls, use established outhouse facilities whenever possible. If these are unavailable, bury human waste 6 to 8 inches deep and pack out used toilet paper. This is a good reason to carry a lightweight trowel. Keep waste at least 300 feet away from any surface water or boggy spots.

Strictly follow the pack-it-in/pack-it-out rule. If you carry something into the wilderness, consume it completely or carry it out with you. Take nothing but pictures; leave with nothing but memories. Additionally, it is important to note that federal law prohibits disturbing historical and archaeological sites. Do not disturb or remove any objects from the trails.

More general trail etiquette includes moving off the trail for less mobile trail users. Where dogs are permitted on trails, keep them leashed and follow all posted guidelines at the trailhead. If you encounter horseback riders, step downhill on the trail and talk in a normal voice to the riders—this calms the horses.

Leave No Trace—put your ear to the ground in the wilderness and listen carefully. Thousands of people coming behind you are thanking you for your courtesy and good sense.

Safety and Preparation

Aside from following the Leave No Trace principles, it is imperative that hikers keep in mind the potential natural hazards of hiking in the Santa Fe area. Forest fires have left some of the areas surrounding the trails scarred—with several implications. Unstable ground is common in areas recently burned. Hazard trees—trees that are leaning, broken, or dead—can be easily toppled by the wind, so beware during times of windy weather.

Next, it must be noted that the possibility of encountering rattlesnakes is very legitimate. While encounters are rare and usually pleasantly uneventful—and nearly unheard of above 8,000 feet in elevation—watch where you put your hands and feet. Never try to touch, move, or capture rattlesnakes. The guidelines for rattlesnake bite treatment are endless, but the common denominator is: Seek medical attention immediately.

While the climate of Santa Fe is nearly ideal for year-round hiking, it is essential to note the weather patterns of the monsoon season, which begins in July. The monsoon season brings powerful afternoon thunderstorms as a result of cloud buildup in the morning. Plan hiking trips so you are not left exposed on peaks or ridgetops on summer afternoons. Seek lower ground before storms start, and beware of lightning.

Another complication of late afternoon thunderstorms is flash flooding. While most of the drainages, arroyos, and creek beds along the trails are normally dry, intense rainfall can result in flash floods in any stream channel. Be very aware of weather conditions during the monsoon season especially, and avoid these areas if rain is likely, and particularly if it is raining. Be mindful that storms on top of a watershed can result in high water many miles downstream. Lastly, never enter the floodwaters should a flash flood occur during a hike.

Beyond the hazards on the trails themselves and the weather patterns of monsoon season, you ought to be prepared for the effects Santa Fe's location has on the body. The high elevation, latitude, and aridity of Santa Fe intensify the sun's ultraviolet radiation, which can lead to quick sunburn. To avoid sun exposure, wear plenty of sunscreen, a hat, and appropriate clothing. Drink plenty of water to avoid heat cramps, exhaustion, dehydration, and heat stroke. Drink water before you feel thirsty and carry enough to drink about one cup of water per mile hiked. Additionally, plan hikes to avoid being on exposed trails in the strongest sun at midday. Hike early in the morning or late in the afternoon.

Aside from plenty of water and sunscreen, come prepared with a high-protein snack, a first aid kit, layered clothing, and a rain jacket. You may want to consider bringing hiking sticks for hikes with a greater elevation gain, especially as they are known to significantly decrease impact on knees. Be sure to tell someone where you are going and when you plan to be back before embarking on any hike.

A final yet significant consideration before hiking in the Santa Fe area is the effect of the high elevation. While not common, acute mountain sickness (AMS)—caused by low oxygen content in the blood—can cause headache, dizziness, nausea, fatigue, irritability, and shortness of breath. Severe symptoms are not likely, but can include vomiting, diarrhea, and extreme fatigue. Seek medical attention as soon as possible if severe symptoms occur. The best way to avoid AMS is to take time to allow your body to acclimate to the elevation. One to two days with plenty of rest and water usually ensures avoidance of symptoms.

Please do not allow these precautions and guidelines to deter you from exploring the abundant beauty and variety that Santa Fe-area hiking has to offer. While each of the hazards and risks is possible, most are rarely problematic for hikers at any time of year. With a variety of terrain available year-round, the rewards easily surpass the risks. A complete anthology of the best hikes in Santa Fe would span hundreds of pages, but we hope this guidebook provides an introduction to the area and its opportunities, encouraging further exploration and investigation.

Map Legend

25	Interstate Highway
84	US Highway
14	State Highway
	Local Road
======	Unpaved Road
- - - - -	Unimproved Road
▬▬▬▬▬	Featured Trail
- - - - - -	Trail
	River/Creek
	Intermittent Stream
⬭	Body of Water
	National Park/Forest/Monument
	Indian Reservation
	State/Local Park
⌐	Bench
▲	Camping
✪	Capital
∩	Cave
⌶	Gate
▲	Mountain/Peak
🅿	Parking
🅰	Picnic Area
■	Point of Interest/Structure
🚐	RV Park
🎿	Ski Area
○	Town
❶	Trailhead
🗺	Viewpoint/Overlook
❓	Visitor/Information Center
≋	Waterfall

Santa Fe

Santa Fe represents a unique blend of Spanish, Mexican, American Indian, and North American cultures, all of which permeate every aspect of life and activity in northern New Mexico.

Urban trails have recently been developed in many cities, and Santa Fe is no exception. The Santa Fe Foothill Trails system has, at present, 34 miles of hiking and biking trails, extending across land owned by Santa Fe County, the City of Santa Fe, the USDA Forest Service, The Nature Conservancy, and private land. We have included several of these trails in this edition.

Other hikes are located in the Sangre de Cristo Mountains, adjacent to Santa Fe. Named the "blood of Christ" because of their color at sunset, these mountains have the highest elevation of any range in New Mexico, and are the southernmost subrange of the Rocky Mountains.

Because of their proximity to Santa Fe, many of these hikes are frequently busier after work hours and on weekends. The trails are well worn and well maintained, serving not only hikers but also runners, mountain bikers, and many a dog.

We have also included hikes that are not in the immediate Santa Fe area but are within easy driving distance, the farthest being about 35 miles. We believe they definitely fit into our mission of "best" and "easy," and are well worth the extra mileage and time.

1 Black Canyon Trail

This hike, close to Santa Fe, is suitable for children, well shaded, and a good introduction to the mountain terrain, fir-aspen belt vegetation, and wildflowers of this elevation in the Sangre de Cristo Mountains. The trailhead is located in newly renovated Santa Fe National Forest's Black Canyon Campground, where half of the campsites can be reserved: www.recreation.gov; (877) 444-6777. Camping here is a real treat!

Distance: 2.1-mile loop
Ascent: 342 feet
Hiking time: About 45 minutes
Difficulty: Easy
Trail surface: Dirt and rock forest trail
Best season: Spring, summer, fall
Other trail users: "With the exception of designated wilderness, most National Forest trails are open to mountain biking."
Canine compatibility: Leashed dogs permitted
Fees and permits: None
Schedule: Year-round access

Maps: USGS McClure Reservoir NM; USDA Forest Service Santa Fe National Forest map. Santa Fe Mountains Trail Map, Map Adventures Maps & Guides, available at Travel Bug, 839 Paseo de Peralta, Santa Fe; (505) 992-0418; www.mapsofnewmexico.com
Trail contact: Santa Fe National Forest; (505) 438-5300. Santa Fe National Forest Espanola Ranger District; (505) 753-7331; www.fs.usda.gov/santafe
Special considerations: Can be icy in winter

Finding the trailhead: From Santa Fe Plaza, head north on Washington Avenue. At the first light after the intersection with Paseo de Peralta, turn right onto Artist's Road, which becomes NM 475. At approximately 7 miles turn right (east) into Black Canyon

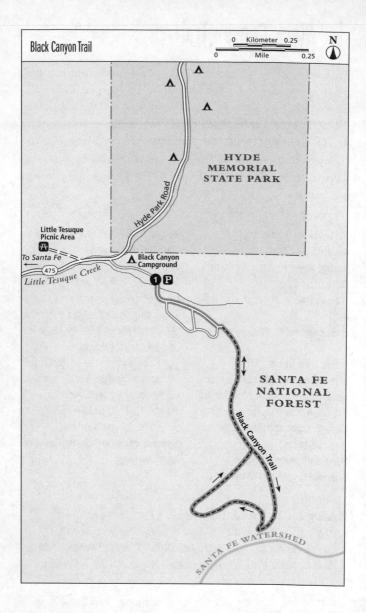

Black Canyon Trail

Kilometer 0.25

Mile 0.25

N

Little Tesuque
Picnic Area

To Santa Fe

475

Little Tesuque Creek

Black Canyon
Campground

1 P

Hyde Park Road

HYDE
MEMORIAL
STATE PARK

SANTA FE
NATIONAL
FOREST

Black Canyon Trail

SANTA FE WATERSHED

Campground. Parking is allocated for hikers on the left, immediately before the campground entrance. Hike through the campground to the far end of loop, and the trailhead is located between campsite 24 and the bathrooms. GPS: N35 43.32' / W105 50.8'

The Hike

The first section of the hike is a gradual ascent on a wide, somewhat rocky path. At about 0.3 mile there is a sign displaying a double arrow. Proceed left (southeast) for the Black Canyon Loop. The trail veers immediately to the right to ascend through a lightly wooded area. At about 0.7 mile a signpost points in the direction from which you came. Disregard and continue hiking straight. Be certain to stay on the trail, as the Santa Fe watershed is to your left and is out of bounds to hikers. A heavy fine is imposed for trespassing. As you descend for the final part of this loop trail, the trail widens, and felled trees appear on both sides. At 1.2 miles you are back at the double arrow sign. Retrace your steps to the campground.

2 Santa Fe Canyon Preserve Interpretive Trail

This hike, tucked into the Santa Fe River canyon in the bed of a former reservoir, is very close to downtown Santa Fe and is suitable for children. With 190 acres of open space in a thriving bosque of cottonwood and willows, it is one of the last unspoiled riparian areas along the Santa Fe River. Under the ownership and management of The Nature Conservancy, there have been increasing efforts at beaver habitat restoration, and sightings are increasingly common. In addition, 140 species of birds have been found among the wetlands and ephemeral pools.

Distance: 1.5-mile loop
Ascent: 175 feet
Hiking time: About 45 minutes
Difficulty: Easy
Trail surface: Dirt
Best season: All seasons, but can get icy in winter and muddy in summer
Other trail users: None; bikes not permitted
Canine compatibility: Dogs not permitted
Fees and permits: None
Schedule: Open year-round, dawn to dusk

Maps: USGS Santa Fe; The Nature Conservancy, www.nature .org; pick up Dale Ball Trails and Connecting Trails maps at Santa Fe Convention and Visitors Bureau, 201 W. Marcy St., Santa Fe (505-955-6200) or download at www.santafe.org or www.santa fenm.gov. Santa Fe City Trails Map (Map Adventures Maps and Guides) is available at Travel Bug, 839 Paseo de Peralta, Santa Fe (505-992-0418), www.mapsof newmexico.com.

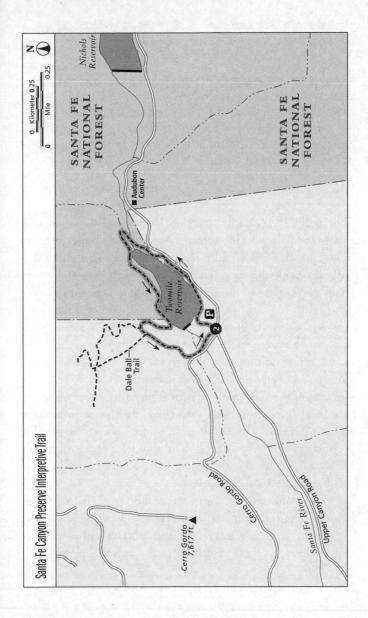

Santa Fe Canyon Preserve Interpretive Trail

N

Cerro Gordo
7,617 ft. ▲

SANTA FE
NATIONAL
FOREST

Nichols
Reservoir

Audubon
Center

Twomile
Reservoir

Dale Ball
Trail

SANTA FE
NATIONAL
FOREST

Cerro Gordo Road

Santa Fe River

Upper Canyon Road

P
2

0   Kilometer 0.25
0   Mile   0.25

Trail contact: The Nature Con-   Santa Fe, NM 87505; (505)
servancy, 212 E. Marcy St. #20,   988-3867

Finding the trailhead: From Santa Fe Plaza drive east on W. San
Francisco Street. Turn right onto Cathedral Place, then turn left onto E.
Alameda St.; drive for about 1.3 miles and turn left on Upper Canyon
Rd. Drive for approximately 1 mile to the intersection of Cerro Gordo
Road on the left. Turn left, and immediately on the right is a parking
lot and the preserve entrance. GPS: N35 41.11' / W105 53.42'

The Hike

The trailhead is clearly visible at the east end of the parking
lot. Immediately an interpretive sign provides both historical
and ecological information on the preserve. This is the first
of many along this loop trail. Head northeast on a well-worn
trail. As you hike, moisture-dependent cottonwoods, wil-
low, and box elder line the riparian area. The trail meanders
beside the stream, comes to a clearing in the willows, takes
a right (heading south), and proceeds uphill for a short distance before coming to a fork in the trail. Walk to your left.
You will see another historical marker, which describes the
features of the old waterworks in front of you. Veering to the
left (north), you will walk through a short, swampy area (in
the springtime), and at the edge of the dam, three benches
provide a great resting place. The trail then heads northeast
along a stone-lined path and comes to another interpretative
plaque at the 0.5-mile marker.

The trail heads left (northwest) and uphill. It then turns
south, along the old metal retaining wall above the reservoir.
When the wall ends, follow the well-marked trail as it curves
north through a gate and then heads into dry arroyos and

piñon hillsides. Shortly beyond the 1-mile mark, you will come upon a sign indicating Dale Ball and Santa Fe Canyon Preserve Trails. Head left to follow the Dale Ball Trail for the last leg of the hike. You will end up on Cerro Gordo Road, where the parking area is located. Turn left to return to the trailhead.

3 Dorothy Stewart Trail

This is a wonderful urban trail, easy to follow and well maintained. The piñon–juniper vegetation is very representative of the Sangre de Cristo foothills, and there are marvelous views in all directions, all with very little exertion. It makes an excellent sunset or evening hike in the summer; however, it can be a real scorcher during the day.

Distance: 2-mile lollipop
Ascent: 437 feet
Hiking time: About 1 hour
Difficulty: Easy
Trail surface: Dirt, rock
Best season: Year-round; may be snowy and icy in winter
Other trail users: Mountain bikers
Canine compatibility: Leashed dogs permitted
Fees and permits: None
Schedule: Year-round
Maps: USGS Santa Fe; pick up Dale Ball Trails and Connecting Trails maps at Santa Fe Convention and Visitors Bureau, 201 W. Marcy St., Santa Fe (505-955-6200) or download at www

.santafe.org or www.santafenm .gov. Santa Fe City Trails Map (Map Adventures Maps and Guides) is available at Travel Bug, 839 Paseo de Peralta, Santa Fe (505-992-0418), www.mapsof newmexico.com.
Trail contact: City of Santa Fe Parks and Recreation Department; (505) 955-2103; www .santafenm.gov/parks_recreation
Special Considerations: Trailhead parking is very limited (4 spaces), so it may be necessary to park in the St. John's College parking lot and walk 0.7 mile uphill on Camino Cruz Blanca to the trailhead on the left.

Finding the trailhead: From downtown Santa Fe, take Alameda Street east (paralleling the Santa Fe River). Turn right (south) on Camino Cabra and continue until it intersects with Camino de Cruz

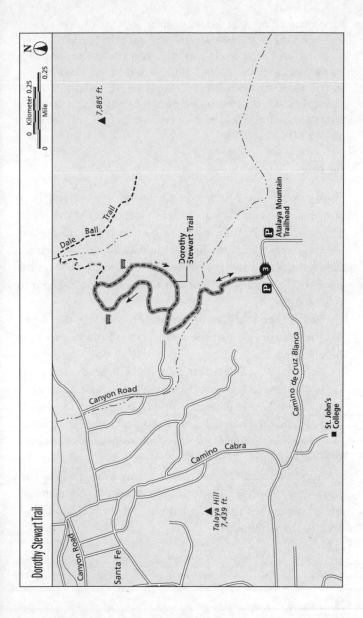

Dorothy Stewart Trail

Dale Ball Trail

Dorothy Stewart Trail

▲ 7,885 ft.

Atalaya Mountain Trailhead

P

P 3

Canyon Road

Canyon Road

Santa Fe

Camino Cabra

Camino de Cruz Blanca

St. John's College

Talaya Hill 7,439 ft.

N

0 Kilometer 0.25
0 Mile 0.25

Blanca. Turn left (west) at this intersection. St. John's College is on your right. Drive for 0.7 mile, and the trailhead is on your left.

If you find it necessary to park at St. John's College and walk to the trailhead, go to the east end of the parking lot and walk a very short distance to a fork in the trail. Hike to the left toward the Dorothy Stewart Trail. After 0.1 mile you will parallel Camino de Cruz Blanca and begin your 0.6 walk uphill on a manicured, gravel sidewalk. GPS: N35 40.14' / W105 54.8'

The Hike

Walk through the opening in the wooden fence and head downhill. Immediately you come to a fork in the trail. Hike left. At about 0.25 mile, near the bottom of a small canyon, the trail takes a turn to the left (northwest), as the sign for the Dorothy Stewart Trail indicates. Be certain to stay on the main trail (a smaller trail cuts off to the left as you begin to walk uphill).

The higher you climb, the more rewarding the views. The first distant view of mountains is the Sandia range near Albuquerque.

At about 0.5 mile the trail splits. Go north (left). The views continue to be spectacular; you will come upon a great log and rock bench. From this point, continue to the 1-mile mark, where the Dale Ball Trail breaks off to the left (northeast). Continue straight ahead on the well-marked Dorothy Stewart Trail loop.

Another bench appears, and this time the view is of Tesuque Peak. Continue on to loop around the mountainside and reconnect with the original trail, which you will follow back to the trailhead.

4 Dale Ball Trail–North

The Dale Ball Trail–North is only one of many hiking and biking trails in the Dale Ball system. It is close to Santa Fe and gives a good introduction to the piñon and juniper hillsides, as well as the unusual and diverse seasonal flora that surround the city. Although it meanders through private property at times, it often seems very remote and far from any development. All trails are well laid out to eliminate blind corners and erosion and are well maintained; each has an informative activity board at the trailhead. This can be a great evening hike, but it can be very hot in the summer.

Distance: 3.6-mile loop
Ascent: 584 feet
Hiking time: 1.5 to 2 hours
Difficulty: Moderate
Trail surface: Dirt, rock
Best season: Summer, fall, spring; winter may be icy and snowy
Other trail users: Mountain bikers
Canine compatibility: Leashed dogs permitted. There is a large dog park across the street from the trailhead parking lot.
Fees and permits: None
Schedule: Year-round, from a half-hour before sunrise to a half-hour after sunset

Maps: USGS Santa Fe; pick up Dale Ball Trails and Connecting Trails maps at Santa Fe Convention and Visitors Bureau, 201 W. Marcy St., Santa Fe (505-955-6200) or download at www .santafe.org or www.santafenm .gov. Santa Fe City Trails Map (Map Adventures Maps and Guides) is available at Travel Bug, 839 Paseo de Peralta, Santa Fe (505-992-0418), www.mapsof newmexico.com.
Trail contacts: Santa Fe County Open Space and Trails Division; (505) 992-9873; www.santafecountynm.gov/ open_space_and_trails_program

Special considerations: Because this trail system has been created with easements provided by private property owners, it is requested that you stay on the trail, take no shortcuts (often the easements are only 6 feet wide), be respectful of private property, and be responsible with your dog. Having access to these open spaces is a privilege, which could be lost if abused.

Finding the trailhead: From Santa Fe Plaza drive north on Washington Avenue. At the first light after the intersection with Paseo de Peralta, turn right onto Artists Rd., which becomes NM 475 and Hyde Park Road. Drive 2.6 miles (do not measure mileage by the mile markers) to the junction with the Sierra del Norte development sign, on your left. Turn left and take an immediate right into the parking lot. GPS: N35 42.39' / W105 53.58'

The Hike

Note: There is a map of the entire Dale Ball trail system at the south end of the parking lot.

Begin the hike at the north end of the parking lot. Walk uphill and veer to the left (northwest) through piñon and juniper. At post 2 go right (southeast); the trail then turns to the left (northwest). Ascend on several switchbacks, and you are rewarded with a clear view of the Jemez Mountains to the northeast. There is then a gentle elevation gain, and at about 0.6 mile Black Mesa (adjacent to San Ildefonso Pueblo) can be seen to the west. This mesa is a historic landmark in the Rio Grande Valley.

At about 1.1 miles there is a junction and sign for La Piedra Trail, a 2012 addition to the trail system. Go left. At post 3 go right (south). There is an immediate downhill on long, gentle switchbacks.

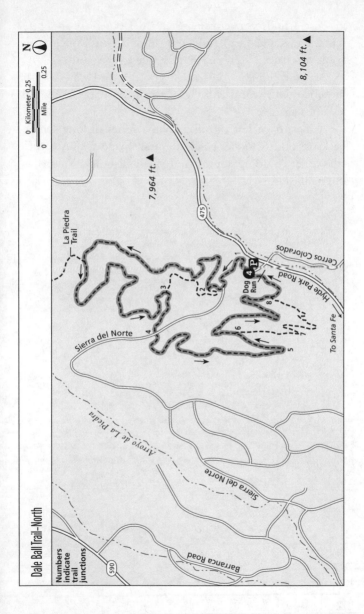

Dale Ball Trail–North

Numbers indicate trail junctions

N

0 Kilometer 0.25

0 Mile 0.25

La Piedra Trail

Sierra del Norte

3

2

4

Dog Run

P

8

6

7

5

Cerros Colorados

Hyde Park Road

To Santa Fe

475

7,964 ft.

8,104 ft.

Arroyo de La Piedra

Sierra del Norte

Barranca Road

590

Post 4 finds you crossing Sierra del Norte at about 1.7 miles. Cross and head right (north) and uphill once again. Soon you have a view of Albuquerque to the south.

At post 5 hike to the left (north), and you will be rewarded with wonderful views across the Rio Grande Valley once again.

At post 6 go left (north), down a series of long switchbacks to post 8 (do not take the trail to post 7). At post 8 take a left (heading south), and you will quickly return to the trailhead.

5 Chamisa Trail

This hike is close to Santa Fe and offers a good workout as well as great exposure to piñon–juniper and mixed conifer vegetation belts. As a summer hike it is shaded much of the day. Although there is an initial climb, you are rewarded with a welcome descent into the Tesuque Creek basin, where you can rest amid cool water, wildflowers, and a green meadow.

Distance: 5.3 miles out and back

Ascent: 1,300 feet

Hiking time: About 2.5 hours

Difficulty: Moderate

Trail surface: Dirt

Best season: Spring (may be icy in early spring), summer, fall

Other trail users: Mountain bikers, runners

Canine compatibility: Leashed dogs permitted.

Fees and permits: None

Schedule: Year-round

Maps: USGS McClure Reservoir and Aspen Basin NM. USDA Forest Service Pecos Wilderness Map. Santa Fe Mountains Map, Map Adventures Maps & Guides, available at Travel Bug, 839 Paseo de Peralta, Santa Fe; (505) 992-0418; www.mapsof newmexico.com

Trail contacts: Santa Fe National Forest, Espanola Ranger District, 1710 N. Riverside Dr., Espanola, NM 87532; (505) 753-7331

Special consideration: This is a popular, highly trafficked trail for mountain bikers, runners, and dogs, especially on weekends.

Finding the trailhead: From Santa Fe Plaza drive north on Washington Avenue. Proceed through the intersection with Paseo de Peralta and turn right at the first light onto Artists Road, which becomes NM 475/Hyde Park Road. At 5.6 miles, large parking areas are on both sides of the road. The trailhead is located at the east end of the parking lot on the left (north). GPS: N35 43.43' / W105 51.57'

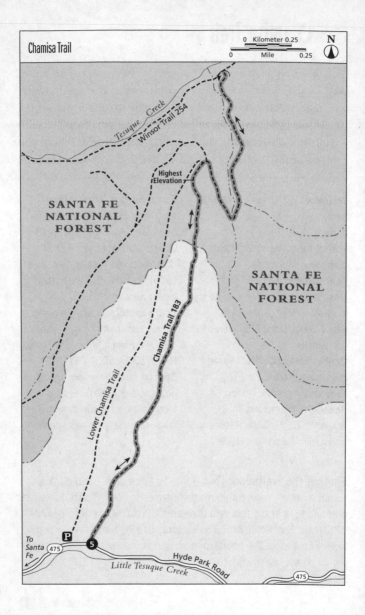

The Hike

The trailhead is marked with a signpost; the trail quickly turns northeast to follow the rim of the canyon. This gradual climb is sunny, warm, and dry in summer, and it may be a good idea to wait for a late-afternoon starting time.

About 1.5 miles from the trailhead, at the top of the ridge, there is a signpost and trail map. You may notice another trail to your left, which is an alternate route from the parking lot. Turn right (southeast) and follow the main trail downhill, descending into a canyon, where the trail parallels a small stream (often dry during years of drought). This portion of the hike can be cool and shaded, and wildflowers thrive when there is water.

At 2.3 miles there are two trail markers on wooden posts, indicating an intersection with Winsor Trail 254. This is the end of Chamisa Trail 183, but look to the right for a pristine meadow, providing a pleasant resting place near the creek, before you retrace your steps.

To return, turn left (south) at the two posted signs near the meadow, and when you reach the saddle be sure to take the trail to the left, retracing your steps to return to the trailhead.

6 Borrego-Bear Wallow-Winsor Triangle Trail

This hike, which uses Borrego Trail 150, Bear Wallow Trail 182, and Winsor Trail 254, is very close to Santa Fe and is a quick getaway to the mountains and streams of the Sangre de Cristos. It's a beautiful fall hike, and popular with runners, dogs, and bikers, so be prepared for all kinds of company, especially on weekends.

Distance: 4.3-mile lollipop
Ascent: 770 feet
Hiking time: About 2 hours
Difficulty: Moderate
Trail surface: Dirt
Best season: Late spring, summer, fall (beautiful with aspens)
Other trail users: Mountain bikers, joggers
Canine compatibility: Leashed dogs permitted. Please pick up after your dog.
Fees and permits: None
Schedule: Year-round

Maps: USGS Aspen Basin NM. USDA Forest Service Pecos Wilderness Map. Santa Fe Mountains Map, Map Adventures Maps & Guides, available at Travel Bug, 839 Paseo de Peralta, Santa Fe; (505) 992-0418; www.mapsof newmexico.com
Trail Contacts: Santa Fe National Forest, Espanola Ranger District;1710 N. Riverside Dr., Espanola, NM 87532; (505) 753-7331

Finding the trailhead: From Santa Fe Plaza drive north on Washington Avenue. Proceed through the intersection with Paseo de Peralta and turn right at the first light onto Artists Road, which becomes NM 475 / Hyde Park Road. Drive 8.5 miles to a parking lot/trailhead on the left side of the road (there is often overflow parking on the highway). GPS: N35 44.46' / W105 50.5'

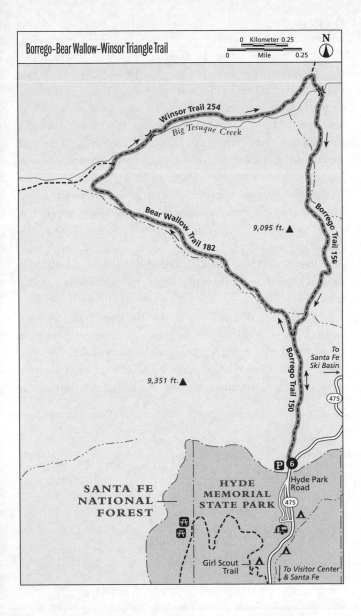

Borrego–Bear Wallow–Winsor Triangle Trail

0   Kilometer   0.25

0   Mile   0.25

N

Winsor Trail 254

Big Tesuque Creek

Borrego Trail 150

9,095 ft. ▲

Bear Wallow Trail 182

9,351 ft. ▲

Borrego Trail 150

To
Santa Fe
Ski Basin

475

P 6 Hyde Park Road

475

SANTA FE
NATIONAL
FOREST

HYDE
MEMORIAL
STATE PARK

Girl Scout
Trail

To Visitor Center
& Santa Fe

The Hike

From the north end of the parking lot, head downhill past the trailhead/map board. Douglas fir, Rocky Mountain maple, and large aspen line this wide, shaded path, once used to herd sheep to market from the north. The trail drops into a drainage, heading north. After an easy 0.5 mile, turn left at the junction of Borrego Trail 150 and Bear Wallow Trail 182, picking up the Bear Wallow Trail. On your return you will loop back to this point on Borrego Trail.

For the next mile follow Bear Wallow Trail to the crossing of Tesuque Creek. Watch for changes in the vegetation, especially on the southern slope, before you reach the stream crossing at about 1.5 miles.

After crossing the creek on the new footbridge, turn right onto Winsor Trail. Follow this wide trail through a wooded area.

At 2.5 miles you will encounter Borrego Trail 150 once again. Turn right (south) to begin the last leg of your hike. Cross the creek on the log bridge. The switchbacks take you back to the Bear Wallow junction at 3.9 miles. Continue straight ahead, retracing your steps back to the trailhead.

7   Hyde Park Circle Trail

This hike is located in Hyde Memorial State Park, New Mexico's oldest and highest-elevation state park. It is situated along the Little Tesuque Creek in the Sangre de Cristo Mountains, very close to Santa Fe. Although there is some steep climbing, the panoramic views of the Jemez, Sandia, San Pedro, Ortiz, and Sangre de Cristo ranges make this hike well worth the effort.

Distance: 3.4-mile loop
Ascent: 1,058 feet
Hiking time: About 2 hours
Difficulty: Difficult due to a steep climb in short distance at the beginning of the hike
Trail surface: Dirt and rock; forested
Best season: Late spring, summer, fall
Other trail users: Runners
Canine compatibility: Leashed dogs permitted
Fees and permits: A per-vehicle day-use fee is charged

Schedule: Trail is open year-round for day use from 6 a.m. to 9 p.m.
Maps: USGS McClure Reservoir and Santa Fe NM. USDA Forest Service Pecos Wilderness Map. Available at Hyde Park Visitor Center on Hyde Park Road; online at www.emnrd.state.nm.us.
Trail contact: Hyde Memorial State Park, 740 Hyde Park Rd., Santa Fe, NM 87501; (505) 983-7175, (888) NM-Parks; www.emnrd.state.nm.us/SPD/hydememorialstatepark.html

Finding the trailhead: From Santa Fe Plaza drive north on Washington Avenue. Proceed through the intersection with Paseo de Peralta and turn right at the first light onto Artists Road, which becomes NM 475/Hyde Park Road. Drive approximately 7.4 miles until you reach the Hyde Memorial State Park Visitor Center on the right side of the

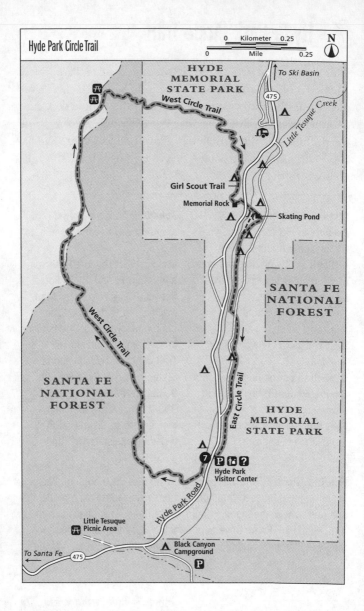

road. Park here and cross the highway to the trailhead. GPS: N35 43.50' / W105 50.15'

The Hike

The trail begins by crossing the bridge over Little Tesuque Creek. Trail guides may be offered in the post by the creek; there were none available when we set out. However, you will find a bulletin board with all trail information at the trailhead.

Head left (south) on West Circle Trail up a rather steep set of switchbacks. You will gain elevation rapidly in this hike, making the first mile, to the top, taxing in places. There is shade on the hike, and the Hyde Park rangers have done a wonderful job maintaining this trail. Also along your ascent are two benches, welcomed resting spots, and the second bench offers great panoramic views.

At the top of the ridge, the trail sign reads 1.23 miles and 1,058 feet in elevation gain. Hike a short while longer to two picnic tables. From this vantage point you can view the Sandia Mountains to the southwest and the Jemez Mountains to the northwest, across the Rio Grande Valley. Begin your descent here on the West Circle Trail.

When you are nearly at the bottom of your descent, there is a sign for Circle Trail. Go right on the switchback and continue until you see a sign for the Girl Scout Trail and Circle Trail. Follow the Girl Scout Trail to the right (uphill). The trail eventually ends at a large memorial rock, at which point the trail crosses the highway.

After you have crossed, locate the East Circle Trail that runs alongside Little Tesuque Creek for a shaded, easy walk on both trail and road, through the campground, back to the Hyde Park Visitor Center and the trailhead.

8 Alamo (Alamos) Vista Trail

This trail is the most recent addition to hikes in the vicinity of the ski area. It originates adjacent to the Aspen Vista parking lot and trailhead. Placed at the trailhead is a plaque, dedicating the trail to an extraordinary young woman, Tessa Horan, who lost her life while serving in the Peace Corps in 2006. This trail is a fitting tribute to her, as it takes the hiker to a beautiful meadow, through stands of amazing aspens, and to mountain views worth all the effort of a rather steep hike.

Distance: 2.4 miles out and back

Ascent: 1,164 feet

Hiking time: About 1.5 hours

Difficulty: Moderately difficult due to steep ascent

Trail surface: Dirt and grass forest path

Best season: Spring, summer, fall

Other trail users: Equestrians

Canine compatibility: Leashed dogs permitted. Please clean up after your dog.

Schedule: Year-round

Maps: Santa Fe Mountains Map, Map Adventures Maps & Guides, available at Travel Bug, 839 Paseo de Peralta, Santa Fe; (505) 992-0418 (trail is shown as "Alamo Vista"); www.mapsof newmexico.com

Trail contact: Santa Fe National Forest, Espanola Ranger District; 1710 N. Riverside Dr., Espanola, NM 87532; (505) 753-7331

Special considerations: At this time, this trail is so new that it is not yet found on USFS or USGS maps. It is sometimes referred to as Alamos Trail.

Finding the trailhead: From Santa Fe Plaza drive north on Washington Avenue. Drive through the intersection with Paseo de Peralta and turn right at the first light onto Artists Road, which becomes NM 475 / Hyde Park Road. Follow the highway for 12.6 miles to Aspen

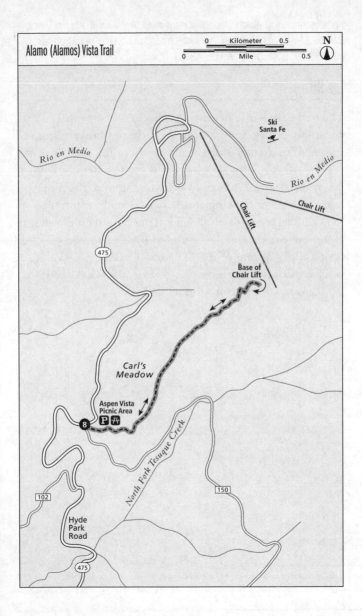

Alamo (Alamos) Vista Trail

Kilometer
0   0.5
Mile
0   0.5

N

Ski Santa Fe

Rio en Medio

Rio en Medio

Chair Lift

475

Chair Lift

Base of Chair Lift

Carl's Meadow

Aspen Vista Picnic Area

8 P

North Fork Tesuque Creek

150

102

Hyde Park Road

475

Vista picnic area, which is on the right side of the road. Alamo Vista Trail begins directly behind the large information sign in the parking lot. GPS: N35 46.38' / W105 48.37'

The Hike

The trail begins in a heavily wooded area of aspens. The forest in July can be very lush in an early and heavy monsoon season. After a fairly steep climb of about 0.5 mile you will enter Carl's Meadow. Look around for wonderful views of the valley below. This could be a turnaround place, or you can continue on the singletrack, narrow, and steep trail.

The final segment of the hike is once again uphill, ending in a more barren area just prior to the turnaround point at the terminus of one of the Ski Santa Fe ski lifts. Once again you have wonderful panoramic views of the Rio Grande Valley. Retrace your steps to the trailhead.

9 Arroyo Hondo Open Space

Arroyo Hondo Open Space consists of 87 acres and is located only about 7.5 miles from Santa Fe Plaza. There are two trailheads and a myriad of trails, all providing excellent views of the Ortiz Mountains, Cerrillos Hills, and Galisteo Basin; from the highest parts of the trail it is possible to see Mount Taylor, more than 100 miles away. The ruins of ancient Arroyo Hondo Pueblo are visible from several points on the trail. Sunset is a favorite time.

Distance: 2.3-mile lollipop
Ascent: 397 feet
Hiking time: About 1.5 hours
Difficulty: Easy
Trail surface: Dirt, rock
Other trail users: Mountain bikers, equestrians
Canine compatibility: Leashed dogs permitted
Fees and permits: None
Schedule: Year-round from dawn to dusk
Maps: USGS Santa Fe; pick up Dale Ball Trails and Connecting Trails #3 maps at Santa Fe Convention and Visitors Bureau, 201 W. Marcy St., Santa Fe (505-955-6200) or download at www.santafenm.gov or from Santa Fe Conservation Trust at www.SFCT.org. Santa Fe City Trails Map (Map Adventures Maps and Guides) is available at Travel Bug, 839 Paseo de Peralta, Santa Fe (505-992-0418), www.mapsofnewmexico.com.
Trail contract: Santa Fe County Open Space and Trails Program, 102 Grant Ave., Santa Fe, NM 87501; (505) 992-9873; www.santafecountynm.gov/open_space_and_trails_program
Special considerations: Exposed areas with little or no shade. Take plenty of water on hot, sunny days, and be mindful of threatening storms during summer monsoons.

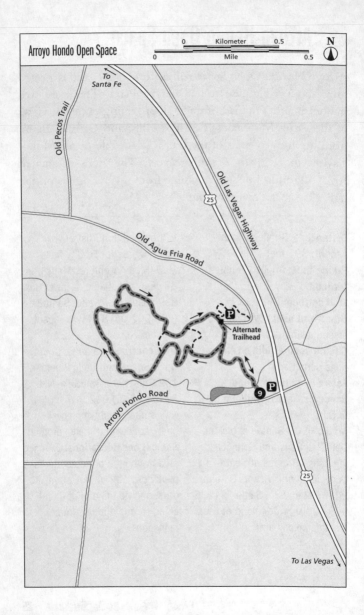

Arroyo Hondo Open Space

Kilometer
0   0.5
Mile
0   0.5

N

To Santa Fe

Old Pecos Trail

Old Las Vegas Highway

25

Old Agua Fria Road

Alternate Trailhead

P

Arroyo Hondo Road

9 P

25

To Las Vegas

Finding the trailhead: From the Santa Fe Plaza turn right onto Cathedral Place. Very quickly turn right onto East Alameda Street, and then make a quick left onto Old Santa Fe Trail. In 2.2 miles turn left onto Old Pecos Trail. After 1.2 miles turn left onto Old Las Vegas Highway. In approximately 1 mile go through the light at El Gancho Way. About 0.3 mile past the light, turn right on Arroyo Hondo Road, and in 0.2 mile turn right into the trailhead parking area, where there are eight parking spaces. GPS: N35 37.13' / W105 55.15'

An alternate trailhead can be found by following the preceding directions to the intersection of Old Pecos Trail and Old Las Vegas Highway. Instead of turning left onto Old Las Vegas Highway, proceed straight ahead for 0.7 mile. Turn left onto West Old Agua Fria Road. You will see a sign for Arroyo Hondo Open Space. The dirt road becomes CR 58D. At about 0.6 mile you will see a "Dead End" sign. The entrance to the trailhead is in about 0.1 mile on the right. You will find ten parking spaces. GPS N35 37.23' / W105 55.19'

The Hike

Begin the hike at the first trailhead detailed above. It is good to note that five signs are placed in this network of trails, showing hikers their exact location, so getting lost is difficult.

The hike begins with a quick descent past the picnic tables to the left, on a rocky and well-defined trail that switchbacks gradually uphill. The first sign at the top offers a left or right option. Go left, toward the panoramic views in the distance. After a short distance you'll come to a map showing your location, and another left/right option. Go left to extend the loop, and gradually switchback downhill though blooming cholla cactuses in summer.

Another sign, make another left and follow a more gradual descent as the trail continues to veer left for a distance though the piñon and juniper.

At approximately 1.4 miles, another sign, another map, another option. Go left. Shortly beyond, at 1.5 miles, reach another junction with a sign and map. Head left to another junction at 1.7 miles. The alternate trailhead is straight ahead, but head uphill to the right. The trail begins to head back to the original starting point.

At 1.9 miles reach the start of the hiking loop. Head left back toward the parking area, which is visible in the distance.

10 Galisteo Basin

Only about 20 minutes from Santa Fe, the Galisteo Basin Preserve is a planned, rural community of approximately 13,000 acres. It will eventually include 50 miles of hiking, biking, and equestrian trails. The trails in this amazing ecosystem are intended to invite exploration by preserve residents and the general public alike. This hike, beginning at the Cowboy Shack, is representative of others in the preserve. It takes you through hills and arroyos filled with cholla cactus, juniper, and piñon, although nothing provides much shade from hot summer sun. There are wonderful views in the distance of mountain ranges near and far.

Distance: 3-mile lollipop
Ascent: 560 feet
Hiking time: About 1.5 hours
Difficulty: Moderate
Trail surface: Dirt, sand, rock
Best season: Year-round
Other trail users: Mountain bikers, equestrians
Canine compatibility: Leashed dogs permitted
Fees and permits: None
Schedule: Year-round, from sunrise to sunset daily
Maps: Available online at www .galisteobasinpreserve.com. Santa Fe City Trails Map, Map

Adventures Maps & Guides, available at Travel Bug, 839 Paseo de Peralta, Santa Fe; (505) 992-0418; www.mapsofnewmexico .com
Trail contact: The Commonweal Conservancy; (505) 982-0071 ext. 102; www.commonwealcon servancy.org
Special considerations: This is rattlesnake country, so be aware and be careful where you place your hands and hiking feet. It can be very hot in the summer. Hike early and be sure to take enough water.

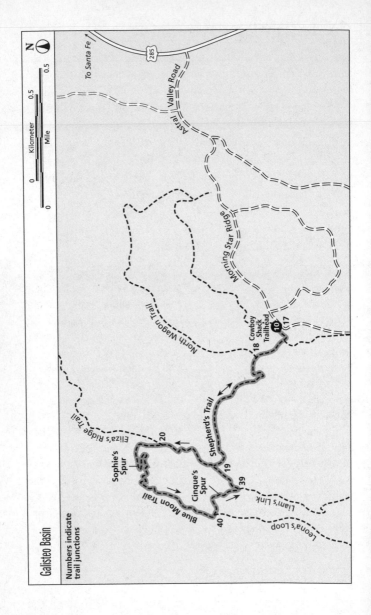

Galisteo Basin

Numbers indicate
trail junctions

To Santa Fe

285

Astra Valley Road

Morning Star Ridge

North Wagon Trail

Cowboy
Shack
Trailhead

10

17

18

Shepherd's Trail

Eliza's Ridge Trail

20

Sophie's Spur

19

Cinque's Spur

Blue Moon Trail

39

40

Liam's Link

Leona's Loop

N

Kilometer   0.5

0   Mile   0.5

Finding the trailhead: From Santa Fe take I-25 north toward Las Vegas. Take exit 290 (US 285) for Clines Corners. Pass El Dorado on your right and the intersection with Avenue Vista Grande. Still on US 285, from here drive 4.3 miles and turn right into the Galisteo Basin Preserve on Astral Valley Road. Drive 1.1 miles on Morning Star Ridge, the main road, to the trailhead at the Cowboy Shack. GPS: N35 28.25' / W105 55.36'

The Hike

The information board at the trailhead provides a clear outline of this hike.

From the sign hike to the right (northwest), past the windmill and water pump on your left and trail marker 17. In a short walk you come to junction 18. Head left onto Shepherds Trail (behind the junction sign with map and mileage) for about 0.7 mile, coming to trail junction 19.

You can go right or left on Eliza's Ridge Trail. For this route, go right. Shortly past this junction the trail follows the top of the ridge with spectacular views.

Reach trail junction 20 at about 1.1 miles. Stay left to begin a loop (going right would continue on Eliza's Ridge).

As you move away from the ridge, there are views of the Ortiz Mountains. As you reach the bottom of the descent, there is a sign with the double arrows. Continue straight ahead, following the arroyo for a few hundred feet, and pick up the trail to the left of the arroyo. This is Blue Moon Trail.

Walk between old fence posts at about 1.7 miles, and the trail then begins to wind through an open area with lush grasses (after an early and very productive monsoon season) and cactuses. After this open area, there is a signpost for junction 40. Go left to head uphill on Cinque's Spur.

In a short while you come to junction 39. This is the junction of Liam's Link and Eliza's Ridge Trails. Hike left (uphill) on Eliza's Ridge Trail to head back toward junction 19 to complete the loop.

At junction 19 head downhill (eastward), back to the parking lot, which you can view in the distance. Pass junction 18 and proceed left, back to the trailhead.

11 La Cieneguilla Petroglyph Site

This short hike is very close to Santa Fe and overlooks a marshy area fed by the San Fe River. It follows a trail paralleling a ridge of low basalt cliffs and allows you to view approximately 4,000 petroglyphs, which are believed to have been placed here in the Pueblo IV period (AD 1350–1600) by Ancestral Pueblo people living in the La Cieneguilla Pueblo south of the petroglyphs. Evidence of the pueblo can be seen from various points on the hike.

Distance: 1.4-mile lollipop
Ascent: 279 feet
Hiking time: About 1.5 hours
Difficultly: Easy
Trail surface: Dirt and rock; requires some boulder scrambling
Other trail users: None, in fact motorized vehicles prohibited
Canine Compatibility: Leashed dogs permitted
Schedule: Year-round from dawn to dusk
Maps: USGS Turquoise Hill quad; New Mexico Bureau of Land Management, State Office, 301 Dinosaur Trail, Santa Fe; (505) 954-2000; download map at

www.blm.gov/nm/st/en/prog/recreation/taos/la_cieneguilla.html
Trail contact: BLM Taos Field Office, 226 Cruz Alta Rd., Taos, NM 87571-5983; (575) 758-8851; www.blm.gov/nm/st/en/fo/Taos_Field_Office.html
Special considerations: This is rattlesnake territory. Be aware and be careful where you place your hands and feet.

Due to the fragility of these petroglyphs, do not climb, touch, or do rubbings, as any direct contact may result in irreparable damage.

Finding the trailhead: From downtown Santa Fe, head east on San Francisco Street, toward the Cathedral. Turn right onto Cathedral Place and turn right again on East Alameda Street. Drive 1 mile and

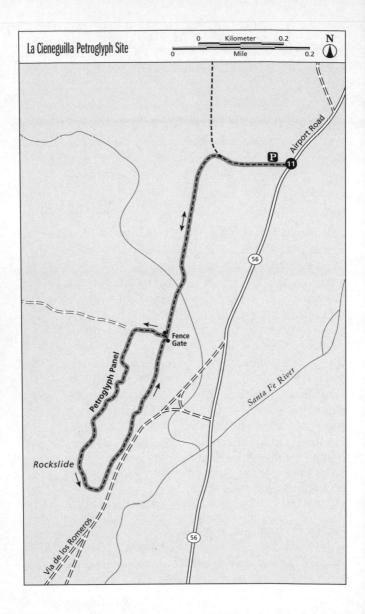

turn left onto St. Francis Drive. After 0.8 mile bear right onto Cerrillos Road and drive 4.4 miles at which point turn right onto Airport Road. The trailhead is 6.6 miles on the right. Airport Road becomes Santa Fe County Road 56 as it leaves Santa Fe city limits. Parking for the trailhead is on the right. It is a short walk to the actual trailhead. GPS: N35 36.31' / W106 7.12.3'

The Hike

There is a very informative BLM interpretive sign at the point where the trail begins. This is an area of historical importance for both ancient Native American villages located nearby and, later, for Spanish migration on the El Camino Real.

Hike left (west) at the sign and along the fence line for about 0.5 mile. Enter through the opening in the fence and walk straight up the escarpment, following the arrow. The trail will bring you just below and parallel to the rim, and you will hike south past panel after panel of humpbacked flute players, spirals, animal and bird images, and many more fascinating symbols.

When you reach a major rockslide, head downhill. At the bottom go left (north) and follow the fence until you return to the original trail, where you will retrace your steps back to the trailhead.

12 Lower Rio en Medio Trail

This is a destination hike to a beautiful waterfall in the foothills of the Sangre de Cristo Mountains. The village of En Medio is located about 6 miles northeast of Tesuque, very close to Santa Fe. The trail follows the Rio en Medio through riparian areas, by drier areas with cactus, and past large Douglas fir. It's suitable for children, who will certainly enjoy the stream crossings.

Distance: 4 miles out and back
Ascent: 800 feet
Hiking time: About 2.5 hours
Difficulty: Moderate
Trail surface: Dirt road, dirt path, several stream crossings and hiking in streambed over rocks
Best season: Spring, summer, fall. The trail is beautiful in winter, but can be very icy.
Other trail users: Equestrians, mountain bikers
Canine compatibility: Leashed dogs permitted
Fees and permits: None
Schedule: All day, year-round
Maps: USGS Aspen Basin quad. USDA Forest Service Pecos

Wilderness Map. Santa Fe Mountains Map by Map Adventures Maps & Guides and Sky Terrain Trail Map of Santa Fe, Bandelier, and Los Alamos, both available at Travel Bug, 839 Paseo de Peralta, Santa Fe; (505) 992-0418; www.mapsofnewmexico.com
Trail contact: Santa Fe National Forest, Espanola Ranger District; 1710 N. Riverside Dr., Espanola, NM 87532; (505) 753-7331
Special considerations: The parking lot at the trailhead has very limited space, and you may be forced to park on the road before the trailhead. Prepare for wet feet.

Finding the trailhead: From downtown Santa Fe, take US 84/285 north, passing the Santa Fe Opera and Tesuque Flea Market exits. Take exit 172, turn right and drive about 0.25 mile. Turn left onto NM

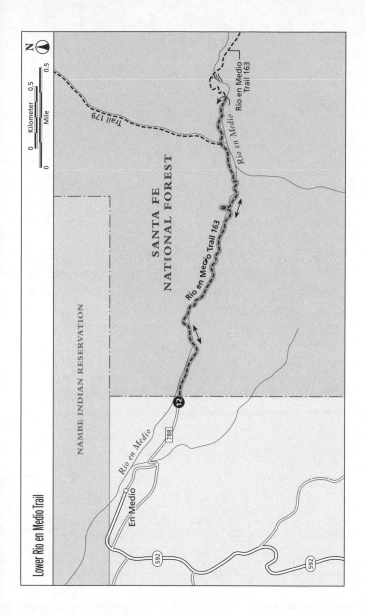

Lower Rio en Medio Trail

NAMBE INDIAN RESERVATION

SANTA FE NATIONAL FOREST

Rio en Medio

En Medio

592

788

12

Rio en Medio Trail 163

Trail 179

Rio en Medio Trail 163

592

N

0   Kilometer   0.5

0   Mile   0.5

592. Drive approximately 3.3 miles and turn left at the stop sign. Follow the road through the small village of En Medio. From the point where the road narrows, the trailhead and parking area are 0.75 mile ahead. GPS: N35 49.16' / W105 53.36'

The Hike

The hike begins on a private dirt road. Walk up the canyon, watching for a trail to the right (Rio en Medio Trail 163). At this point the trail is on private property.

At 0.5 mile from the trailhead, make your first stream crossing. You will be in an open area. At 0.8 mile you will encounter another crossing. At this point you should be on the right side of the stream. Hike to the left.

At 1.1 miles there is a sign for Trail 179 (to the left) and Rio en Medio Trail 163. Stay to the right (on the right side of the stream) to continue toward the waterfall.

Remain on the right side, and at approximately 1.8 miles there is a rocky ascent. Look to the left for a path that takes you down to the creek. Walk upstream a short distance in the creek until you arrive at the waterfall. The last 0.25 mile requires careful footwork on wet rocks in the streambed.

Rest in the shaded and humid area surrounding this beautiful waterfall, and then retrace your steps back to the trailhead.

13 Diablo Canyon

The dramatic basalt cliffs of Diablo Canyon make this a popular hiking and climbing destination in the Santa Fe area. The hike does not follow a trail but a sandy arroyo, which takes you to the Rio Grande in beautiful White Rock Canyon. There is a free campground at the parking area; however, there are neither restrooms nor water.

Distance: 6.3 miles out and back

Ascent: 400 feet

Hiking time: About 3 hours

Difficulty: Moderate

Trail surface: Sandy arroyo

Best season: Winter, early spring, late fall

Other trail users: Climbers, equestrians, ATVs

Canine compatibility: Dogs permitted

Fees and permits: None. Camping is free.

Schedule: Year-round

Maps: USGS White Rock NM (Caja del Rio Canyon). Bureau of Land Management's Los Alamos map. Caja del Rio Plateau Map (Caja del Rio Canyon), Otowi Crossing Press, available at the BLM Information Office, 301 Dinosaur Trail, Santa Fe; (505) 954-2000; www.fs.usda.gov/santafe

Trail contacts: Bureau of Land Management, Taos Field Office, 226 Cruz Alta Rd., Taos, NM 87571; (505) 758-8851; www.blm.gov/nm/st/en/fo/Taos_Field_Office.html. Santa Fe National Forest, Espanola Ranger District; 1710 N. Riverside Dr., Espanola, NM 87532; (505) 753-7331

Special considerations: This hike can be very hot in summer, and there is very little shade. If you choose to go at this time, leave very early in the morning, take lots of water and even a parasol. At any time of year, be aware of weather, as flash flooding does occur in this arroyo.

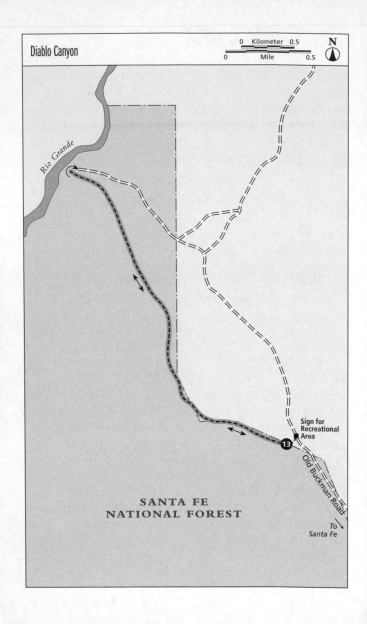

Diablo Canyon

0   Kilometer   0.5
0   Mile   0.5

N

Rio Grande

Sign for
Recreational
Area

13

Old Buckman Road

To
Santa Fe

SANTA FE
NATIONAL FOREST

Finding the trailhead: From Santa Fe, access the Veterans Memorial Highway (NM 599). Take the Camino La Tierra Road exit, heading west. Set your odometer. After about 4 miles, turn right onto Old Buckman Road, a dirt road with its share of washboards! When you have reached a total of 12 miles, there is a sign for Diablo Canyon Recreational Area to your left. Turn here into a well-maintained trailhead parking lot and primitive camping area. Walk west along the fence line until you reach a wooden entrance maze, the start of the hike. GPS: N35 48.22' / W106 8.6'

The Hike

Hike west into the arroyo and canyon. You will walk past beautiful basalt cliffs rising some 300 feet, and you may be able to see a climber or two carefully working up the cliffs. Not far into the arroyo you will be surprised to see a pretty patch of greenery, as a small spring seeps from the sand. The trail takes some turns, and you will do a bit of rock dodging and climbing. The arroyo opens up as you continue to walk toward the river, and the popular Buckman Mesa hike can be seen to your right. Make your way to the Rio Grande, where you will find the shade you may be seeking. After resting retrace your steps back to the trailhead.

14 Cerrillos Hills State Park

Located approximately 16 miles south of Santa Fe, this hike is but one option among many interconnecting trails in a historic mining area (with over 1,100 years of mining history). The park has abandoned mines, one after another, in dry piñon and juniper hills. There are still three operating turquoise mines in the Cerrillos Hills outside the park. The landscape is quiet and offers wonderful views of surrounding mountains ranges. The trails are well maintained and clearly marked.

Distance: 4.8-mile loop
Ascent: 850 feet
Hiking time: About 2.5 hours
Difficulty: Moderate
Trail surface: Wide; sand and rock
Best season: Year-round. Summer can be hot; winter offers great hiking
Other trail users: Equestrians, mountain bikes
Canine compatibility: Leashed dogs permitted
Fees and permits: A daily entrance fee is charged. Use the permit envelopes to deposit your fee and place the white portion on your vehicle. A day-use pass, good for one year at all 35 New Mexico state parks, is available from any ranger.

Schedule: Year-round for day use only
Maps: Park map available at the trailhead and at the visitor center at 37 Main St. in Cerrillos. Available online at www.emnrd.state.nm.us and www.sfct.org/trails-map
Trail contact: Cerrillos Hills State Park, 37 Main St., Cerrillos, NM 87010; (505) 474-0196; www.emnrd.state.nm.us
Special considerations: Yield to horseback riders by stepping off the trail on the downhill side and making sure you are visible. Rock collecting and metal detecting are not allowed. This is rattlesnake country. Be sure to be aware and watch where you put your hands and feet.

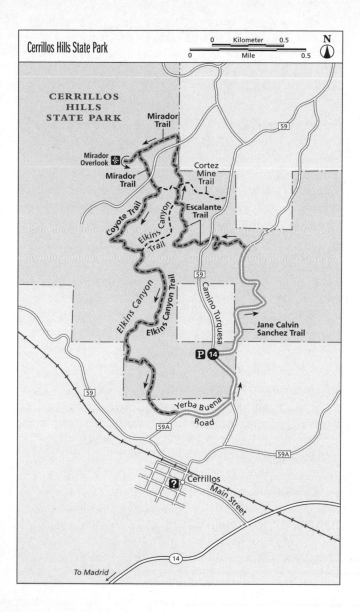

On your way to the trailhead, you may wish to visit the visitor center in the historic village of Cerrillos. It is located in the center of the village at 37 Main St. Pick up a program guide to take advantage of wonderful educational opportunities offered all summer.

Finding the trailhead: From Santa Fe take I-25 south toward Albuquerque. Take exit 278A/NM 14 south toward Madrid for 23.5 miles. Turn right immediately after the railroad overpass to the village of Cerrillos. As you enter the village, take a right at the first intersection. Follow signs for Cerrillos State Park (NM 59) for 0.7 miles to the trailhead. The trailhead is equipped with restrooms, an informational kiosk, and horse trailer parking. GPS: N35 26.40' / W106 7.21'

The Hike

As you will see by consulting the map available at the trailhead, there are many hiking options for Cerrillos Hills. Start this hike across the street from the parking lot. Begin on the Jane Calvin Sanchez Trail, walking uphill for approximately 1 mile (notice two mine shafts along the way). The trail then heads downhill and ends at a road (Camino Turquesa) by the Yoh Toh Mineral Spring.

At this point you can turn left and return to the trailhead following Camino Turquesa (approximately 0.5 mile) or you can turn left, following the road a short distance, where you will see a sign on the right, pointing the way to the Escalante Trail. Follow the arrow to the right, and this trail will very quickly veer north.

You then will reach the intersection of Elkins Canyon Trail and Escalante Trail. Stay on Escalante and pass the intersections with Coyote Trail on the left and Cortez Mine Trail on the right. Continue on Escalante, and on the left you will see a sign for "Escalante View." It's a short distance to this overlook and well worth your time.

Return to Escalante Trail, head to the left, and you will come to a road that is crossed by a fence, which marks the park boundary. Turn sharply to the left and follow the sign to Mirador Trail. In about 0.5 mile again follow a sign to the short Mirador Spur Trail overlook, which gives excellent views of the mountain ranges surrounding Cerrillos.

Return to the main Mirador Trail and continue south (right) on Mirador Trail. Go downhill for just a short distance, until you reach the junction with Coyote Trail. Hike to the right and continue on Coyote Trail. You will soon see a sign that tells the story of Stephen Elkins, and also a steel footbridge over the Pride of the Camp Mine. This is another interesting stop.

Continue on Coyote Trail. Shortly you will reach an intersection; stay to the right, where the trail proceeds downhill, into an arroy, still on Coyote Trail. There are several historic mine shafts along the trail.

Continue downhill to the junction with the Elkins Trail. Hike right on the Elkins Trail. There are several vista points as this trail proceeds slowly downhill, descending into Elkins Canyon.

As the canyon walls diminish, look for a trail veering to the left out of the canyon. This is not marked, so be aware. Take this trail. It ends at a fence and Yerba Buena Road. Turn left onto Yerba Buena Road, and in approximately 0.25 mile you will reach Camino Turquesa Road, which is the road on which you entered the park. A sign points left, indicating the way to a path taking you through the arroyo and back to the parking lot.

15 Kasha-Katuwe Tent Rocks National Monument

Located on the Pajarito Plateau 35 miles south of Santa Fe, the Kasha–Katuwe Tent Rocks National Monument is a unique geological wonder, with cone-shaped formations that are the products of volcanic eruptions that occurred six to seven million years ago. The slot canyon, located not far from the trailhead, is another geological feature not often found in New Mexico. Two hiking trails in the monument provide both easy (Cave Loop Trail) and more difficult (Canyon Trail) access to this area.

Distance: 3.3 miles for the combined Cave Loop Trail and Canyon Trail

Ascent: 922 feet

Hiking time: About 2 hours

Difficulty: Moderate

Trail surface: Dirt, sand, rock, some boulders

Best season: Year-round; can be icy in winter

Other trail users: None

Canine compatibility: Dogs are not permitted

Fees and permits: A fee is levied per vehicle; group, senior, annual, and military annual passes are available

Schedule: Day use only. Fall/winter (Nov 1–Mar 10) from 8 a.m. to 5 p.m. (gate closes at 4 p.m.); spring/summer (Mar 11–Oct 31) from 7 a.m. to 7 p.m. (gate closes at 6 p.m.) The monument may be closed at the request of the Pueblo de Cochiti Tribal Governor for religious observances.

Maps: USGS Canada NM; printable map available at www.blm .gov; trail guide available at the monument entrance

Trail contacts: Bureau of Land Management Albuquerque District, Rio Puerco Field Office, 435 Montano NE, Albuquerque, NM 87101; (505) 761-8955; www .blm.gov. Kasha–Katuwe Tent Rocks National Monument, 435 Montano NE, Albuquerque, NM

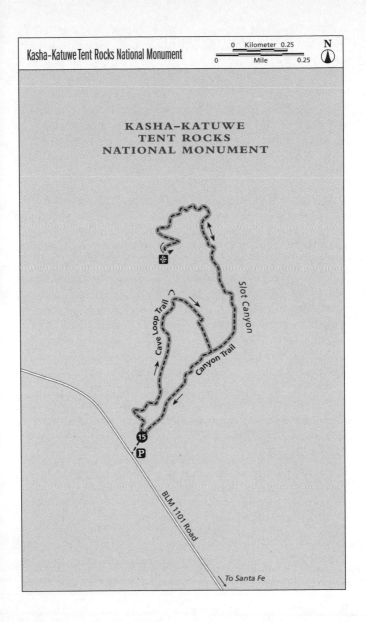

Kasha-Katuwe Tent Rocks National Monument

KASHA–KATUWE
TENT ROCKS
NATIONAL MONUMENT

Cave Loop Trail

Slot Canyon

Canyon Trail

15

P

BLM 1101 Road

To Santa Fe

N

87107; (505) 331-6259; www
.blm.gov/pgdata/content/nm/
en/prog/NLCS/KKTR_NM.html.
Pueblo de Cochiti, 255 Cochiti
St., Cochiti Pueblo, NM 87072;
(505) 465-2244; www.pueblode
cochiti.org

Special considerations: These
trails can be very hot in summer.
There is no water available at
the monument, so plan accord-
ingly. During rainy weather and
thunderstorms, floods may occur
in the canyon. The road may wash
out. For information on weather
and road conditions contact
Pueblo de Cochiti. No disturbing
or collecting of plants, rocks, or
wildlife is permitted. A portion
of the 5-mile access road to
the national monument crosses
Pueblo de Cochiti tribal land.
Please respect these landowners
and their property.

Finding the trailhead: From Santa Fe go south on I-25. Take the
Cochiti Pueblo exit (exit 264). Turn right onto NM 16. In about 8 miles
turn right onto NM 22. In 2.7 miles (Cochiti Dam is on your right),
turn left to stay on NM 22. Follow the signs to Cochiti Pueblo and
Kasha-Katuwe Tent Rocks National Monument. From the fee station it
is about 5 miles to the parking area and trailhead. GPS: N35 39.28'
/ W106 24.40'

The Hike

The 1.2-mile Cave Loop Trail is the easiest of the two trails
that make up the longer hike. Start on this trail. From the
information sign hike left, pass one group of cones, curve
around the base of a cliff (be sure to look up), and cross
through some dry washes. Finally you will come to the cave,
an Ancient Puebloan dwelling.

Continue on the trail as it follows the cliffs and then
descends to meet the Canyon Trail. You have a choice here,
to follow the Canyon Trail to the left or hike back to the
trailhead. To complete this route, follow the Canyon Trail left.

The Canyon Trail continues up the arroyo and then becomes a slot canyon. The narrow, curvy walls of many colors make for an exciting and beautiful adventure as you work your way up the canyon, scrambling over rocks and at one point working your way under a large boulder wedged between the walls of the narrow and towering cliffs.

The trail opens up suddenly, and you will work your way up a curving and narrow gorge. The trail ascends rather steeply in some places as it climbs out of the canyon, but is always well worn.

Just before you reach the top of the mesa, the trail forks. Take the trail to the right to finish your climb. Enjoy the views of the Sangre de Cristo, Jemez, and Sandia Mountain ranges, and all the beauty of the tent rocks beneath you, before you retrace your steps to the trailhead. Make sure that you continue straight when you hit the junction with Cave Loop Trail, returning to the trailhead via the Canyon Trail.

Bandelier National Monument

Driving the 48 miles from Santa Fe to Bandelier National Monument offers a unique opportunity not only to view the geological features and breathtaking scenery of this corner of New Mexico, but also to explore the nearby pueblos of Tesuque, Pojoaque, and San Ildefonso, all located adjacent to the highway. In addition, it is well worth your time to stop at the White Rock Overlook, which provides a breathtaking view of White Rock Canyon and the Rio Grande 600 feet below. It is easily located if you turn left at the first stop light in White Rock (coming from Santa Fe) and follow the signs.

Since the first nomadic peoples traveled to this area over 10,000 years ago, Bandelier has held a special place in the history of northern New Mexico. The oral traditions and migration stories of many of the present-day Pueblo people speak of the mesas and canyons of the Pajarito Plateau. From about AD 1150 to the mid-1500s, Bandelier's Frijoles Canyon was the home of these ancient people. No one knows why they decided to leave, but their descendants are now thought to inhabit many of the present-day pueblos of this area.

In 1916 President Woodrow Wilson designated Bandelier a national monument. It has 32,000 acres of land, 90 percent of which is designated wilderness. Altitudes range from 5,330 feet at the Rio Grande to more than 10,000 feet in the Jemez Mountains. There are more than 1,000 ruins within the 50 square miles of Bandelier, many of which can be seen along the more than 70 miles of well-maintained hiking trails.

We have included only five of what we consider "best" and "easy" trails, but be sure to take advantage of all the popular trails, which originate at the visitor center in Frijoles Canyon.

Much of Bandelier was devastated by fires in 2000 and 2011, as well as by floods in 2013. As you hike you will see evidence of these, as well as evidence of the natural restoration that has occurred. These changes have affected hiking in the monument, and the visitor center is the best place to check out the most recent trail conditions.

Entrance fees are charged. Senior and national parks passes are accepted, and a Bandelier National Monument Annual Pass is available for purchase. There are many free fee days, which may be found on the National Park Service's Bandelier website. Consult www.nps.gov/band for more information.

16 Burnt Mesa Trail

Burnt Mesa is a nearly level hike ending before a steep dropoff into a side canyon of Frijoles Canyon. The trail takes you past several rock mound sites, indicating Ancestral Puebloan life on the mesa. Burnt Mesa was one of the small Coalition Period (AD 1175–1325) pueblos, built on the Pajarito Plateau as people migrated from places north and west. It's a beautiful fall hike, and in summer a great hike for seeing wildflowers and birds.

Distance: 5 miles out and back
Ascent: 300 feet
Hiking time: About 2.5 hours
Difficulty: Easy
Trail surface: Good singletrack dirt footpath
Best season: Year-round
Other trail users: Cross-country skiers in winter
Canine compatibility: Dogs not permitted
Fees and permits: Entrance fees are levied.
Schedule: Year-round from dawn to dusk
Maps: USGS Frijoles NM. Park map available online at www.nps.gov/band. Bandelier National Monument by National Geographic/Trails Illustrated. Map available at Bandelier National Monument Visitor Center in Frijoles Canyon. Sky Terrain map to Santa Fe, Bandelier, and Los Alamos, and National Geographic Trails Illustrated Map, Bandelier, both available at Travel Bug, 839 Paseo de Peralta, Santa Fe; (505) 992-0418; www.mapsof newmexico.com
Trail contact: Bandelier National Monument, 15 Entrance Road, Los Alamos, NM 87544-9508; (505) 672-3861, ext. 517; www.nps.gov/band
Special considerations: Do not disturb or remove any artifacts, pottery, rocks, plants, or wildlife.

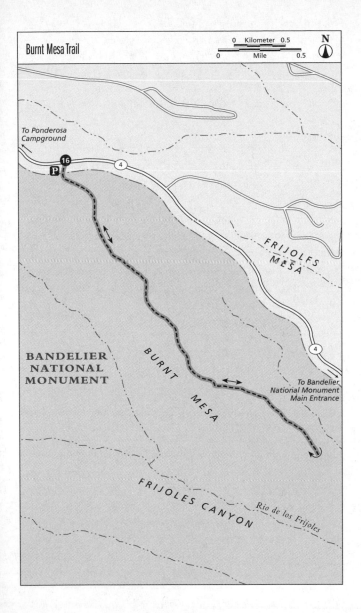

Burnt Mesa Trail

0 Kilometer 0.5

0 Mile 0.5

N

To Ponderosa
Campground

P 16

4

FRIJOLES
MESA

4

BANDELIER
NATIONAL
MONUMENT

BURNT MESA

To Bandelier
National Monument
Main Entrance

FRIJOLES CANYON

Rio de los Frijoles

Finding the trailhead: From Santa Fe, drive north on US 84/285. In Pojoaque, follow signs for Los Alamos and NM 502 for approximately 12 miles, to the junction with NM 4. Take NM 4 south about 12.1 miles, passing the main entrance to Bandelier National Monument. Drive for another 3.9 miles and turn into the trailhead parking area on the left side of the road. GPS: N35 49.69' / W106 19.73'

The Hike

Walk south on the trail, past the interpretive board. The landscape is filled with juniper, oak, and small ponderosa pine.

At about 1 mile the first mound of archaeological rubble can be seen to the right of the trail. The second mound is about 1 mile farther along the trail, and there are two additional mounds about 0.5 mile farther.

Walk to the end of the mesa and enjoy the views of the surrounding canyons before turning around and retracing your route back to the trailhead.

17 Frey Trail

The Frey Trail, once called the Old North Trail, was used by all visitors to Bandelier until 1934, when the Civilian Conservation Corps built the present road. For ten years it was the only trail Mrs. Evelyn Frey (for whom the trail was named) and her husband used as access to their home and guest lodge in Frijoles Canyon. This hike provides an excellent opportunity to obtain an overview of Frijoles Canyon and Tyuonyi Ruin before setting out to explore them in depth. Descend to the canyon bottom on a well-worn trail through meadow, piñon and juniper forest, and finally volcanic rock.

Distance: 4 miles out and back
Ascent: 600 feet
Hiking time: About 2 hours
Difficulty: Moderate
Trail surface: Dirt, sand, and rock
Best season: Year-round. May be hot in summer, as the trail is exposed; in winter it may be snowy and/or icy
Other trail users: None
Canine compatibility: Dogs are not permitted in Bandelier National Monument, with the exception of in Juniper Campground and the picnic area outside the park headquarters in Frijoles Canyon. Your dog must be leashed. The visitor center staff will give you a map showing where you may take dogs on US Department of Energy trails along NM 4 between White Rock and Bandelier. You may also print the map at www.nps.gov/band.
Fees and permits: Entrance fees are levied.
Schedule: Trail open daily, year-round, from dawn to dusk. Frijoles Canyon Visitor Center is open daily from 9 a.m. to 4:30 p.m.
Maps: USGS Frijoles NM map. Park map available at Frijoles Canyon Visitors Center, Sky Terrain map to Santa Fe, Bandelier, and Los Alamos, and National

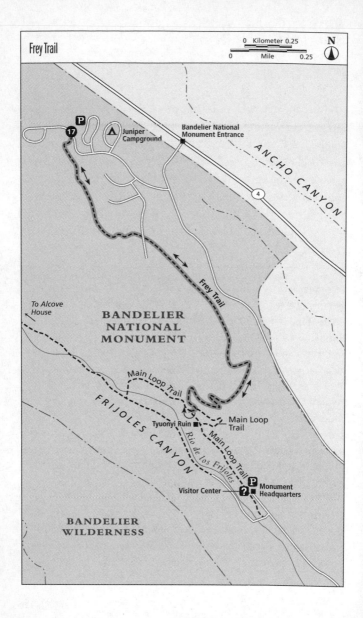

Frey Trail

0   Kilometer 0.25
0   Mile   0.25

N

P
17

Juniper
Campground

Bandelier National
Monument Entrance

ANCHO CANYON

4

Frey Trail

To Alcove
House

BANDELIER
NATIONAL
MONUMENT

Main Loop Trail

FRIJOLES CANYON

Main Loop
Trail

Tyuonyi Ruin

Rio de los Frijoles

Main Loop Trail

Visitor Center

P

?

Monument
Headquarters

BANDELIER
WILDERNESS

Geographic Trails Illustrated Map, Bandelier, both available at Travel Bug, 839 Paseo de Peralta, Santa Fe; (505) 992-0418; www.mapsofnewmexico.com

Trail contact: Bandelier National Monument Headquarters, 15 Entrance Rd., Los Alamos, NM 87544; (505) 672-3861, ext. 517; www.nps.gov/band

Special considerations: This trail is not suitable for small children.

From May 23 to Oct 7 you must travel into Bandelier by shuttle, which departs every 20 minutes from the White Rock Visitor Center (located on NM 4 almost immediately on the right after the first traffic light in White Rock as you drive in from Santa Fe). The White Rock Visitor Center is open from 9 a.m. to 4 p.m. daily; (505) 672-3183.

Finding the trailhead: From Santa Fe take US 285/84 north to Pojoaque. At Pojoaque take NM 502 west, following signs for Los Alamos. Drive approximately 12 miles to the junction with NM 4, following the signs for Bandelier National Monument and White Rock. Drive south on NM 4 for about 12.1 miles. Turn left (south) into the monument entrance (stop to pay the fee). Follow the road a short distance, turning right for Juniper Campground. Drive past the campground registration booth on your right to signs for amphitheater parking on your left. The trailhead is located in the southwest corner of the amphitheater parking lot and is clearly marked. GPS: N35 47.43' / W106 16.53'

The Hike

The trail takes you on a well-worn path through a meadow, then into a more wooded juniper and piñon area. Pass a bench on the right side of the trail after a short distance, and soon after that the trail crosses a road. There is well-marked trail sign on the other side of the road. A gradual descent begins and the trail becomes sandy in this arid landscape.

At about 1 mile you reach the rim of the canyon, and there is a spectacular view to the east. It is a good turnaround point if you are not up for the steep descent or the taxing ascent (about 600 feet) on your return route.

A series of switchbacks takes you to the bottom of the canyon, your destination. However, you will definitely want to take the time to explore the visitor center, the Loop Trail, and possibly even hike to Alcove House. Be sure to obtain a guide at the visitor center, which is easily found by following the main trail to your right or left.

Have a wonderful day of exploration, but be sure to save energy for the ascent back to the trailhead. Return as you came.

18 Frijolito Trail

This short loop trail climbs out of Frijoles Canyon to the mesa top, passes the unexcavated Frijolito Pueblo (thought to have been built between AD 1431 and 1447), winds along the canyon rim, and then drops back into Frijoles Canyon. It offers spectacular views of ruins and cavates, cavelike cliff dwellings, on the north side of the canyon, and of the Jemez Mountains.

Distance: 2.8-mile loop

Ascent: 700 feet

Hiking time: About 1.5 hours

Difficulty: Strenuous due to a steep climb out of Frijoles Canyon

Trail surface: Dirt and rock

Best season: Late spring, summer, fall; icy in winter

Other trail users: None

Canine compatibility: Dogs are not permitted in Bandelier National Monument, with the exception of in Juniper Campground and the picnic area outside the park headquarters in Frijoles Canyon. Your dog must be leashed. The visitor center staff will be happy to give you a map showing where you may take dogs on US Department of Energy trails along NM 4 between White Rock and Bandelier. You may print this map at www.nps.gov/band.

Fees and permits: Entrance fees are levied.

Schedule: Trails open daily, year-round, from dawn to dusk. Frijoles Canyon Visitor Center is open daily from 9 a.m. to 4:30 p.m.

Maps: USGS Frijoles NM. Park map available at Frijoles Canyon Visitors Center. Sky Terrain map to Santa Fe, Bandelier, and Los Alamos, and National Geographic Trails Illustrated Map, Bandelier, both available at Travel Bug, 839 Paseo de Peralta, Santa Fe; (505) 992-0418; www.mapsofnewmexico.com

Trail contact: Bandelier National Monument Headquarters, 15 Entrance Rd., Los Alamos, NM 87544; (505) 672-3861, ext. 517; www.nps.gov/band

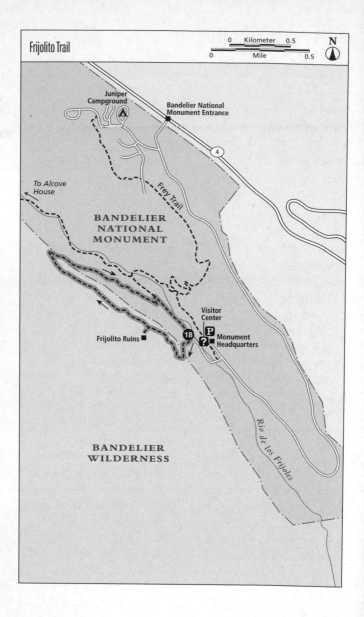

Frijolito Trail

0 — Kilometer — 0.5
0 — Mile — 0.5

N

Juniper Campground

Bandelier National Monument Entrance

4

Frey Trail

To Alcove House

BANDELIER NATIONAL MONUMENT

Visitor Center

P

?

Monument Headquarters

18

Frijolito Ruins

BANDELIER WILDERNESS

Rio de los Frijoles

Special considerations: Between May 23 and Oct 7 you must travel into the park by shuttle. The shuttle departs every 20 minutes from the White Rock Visitor Center (located on NM 4 almost immediately on the right after the first traffic light in White Rock, as you come in from Santa Fe).

The White Rock Visitor Center is open from 9 a.m. to 4 p.m. daily; (505) 672-3183.

Be mindful that this trail can be especially hot in the summer (there is little or no shade), and that there is a steep ascent on switchbacks out of Frijoles Canyon.

Finding the trailhead: From Santa Fe drive north on US 84/285. In Pojoaque follow signs for Los Alamos and NM 502 for approximately 12 miles to the junction with NM 4. Take NM 4 south, through White Rock, for 12.1 miles and turn left, entering Bandelier National Monument. Pass through the entrance station (pay the fee) and proceed straight ahead to the visitor center. Drive down into the canyon, getting a bird's-eye view of Frijoles Canyon looking toward the Rio Grande. GPS: N35 46.44' / W106 16.20'

If you take the shuttle during the high tourist season, you will be dropped off at the visitor center. Walk to the opposite end of the parking lot to the footbridge, where the hike begins.

The Hike

You will find the footbridge crossing Frijoles Creek at the opposite end of the parking lot from the visitor center. Cross the creek and turn right onto the former road to the picnic area (washed away during the 2013 flood). Continue past the old restroom building and the picnic tables on the left, and at the backcountry information sign go left (uphill) to the formal trailhead. There is a sign indicating the mileage to Frijolito Ruins (0.9), Yapashi (5.7), and Painted Cave (10).

Almost immediately there is another sign for Frijolito. Hike left. Here switchbacks begin the steep ascent up the canyon wall.

At about 0.5 mile you will level out on the top of the mesa. Continue north on the trail as it follows the canyon rim for approximately 0.25 mile. You will then see a trail sign on the left for lower Alamo Canyon and the Rio Grande. Turn left here, and in about 400 feet the sign for Frijolito Ruins is on the right.

After visiting the ruins (be sure not to disturb any artifacts), return to the main trail and proceed north (left) for about 1.5 miles. At this point you will see a sign for the visitor center. Take a sharp right to begin a gradual descent on a narrow trail.

Near the bottom of the canyon the trail splits again. The trail straight ahead leads to Alcove House, and the switchback right leads to the visitor center. Go right and continue down the trail to the original junction near the trailhead. Hike left and head down to the formal trailhead, the picnic area road, the footbridge, and on to the trailhead in the parking lot.

19 Tsankawi

Tsankawi is an often overlooked part of Bandelier National Monument, but this short, interesting hike is definitely worth a visit! Located about 12 miles northeast of the main section of the monument, Tsankawi is on top of a narrow mesa. This unexcavated ancient pueblo had, at its peak, about 275 rooms and was probably at least two stories high. It was built around a circular plaza and was occupied during the fifteenth century. With a self-guided tour you will see many cavates (natural cavities in volcanic rock made into large rooms for living space), ancient stairways and paths, petroglyphs, and wonderful views of the Rio Grande valley and mountains beyond.

Distance: 1.8-mile lollipop
Ascent: 281 feet
Hiking time: About 1.5 hours
Difficulty: Moderate
Trail surface: Dirt; narrow passageways in volcanic rock; several ladders
Best season: Year-round, but may be snowy and icy in winter
Other trail users: None
Canine compatibility: Dogs are not allowed in Bandelier National Monument, with the exception of Juniper Campground and the picnic area outside park headquarters in Frijoles Canyon. Your dog must be leashed. The visitor center staff will be happy to give you a map showing where you may take dogs on US Department of Energy trails along NM 4 between White Rock and Bandelier, or you may print the map at www.nps.gov/band.

Fees and permits: An entrance fee is levied. There is a self-serve kiosk at Tsankawi for purchasing passes. Put your pass on your dashboard to avoid being ticketed.

Schedule: Trail open daily, year-round, from dawn to dusk. The Frijoles Canyon Visitor Center is open daily 9 a.m. to 4:30 p.m.

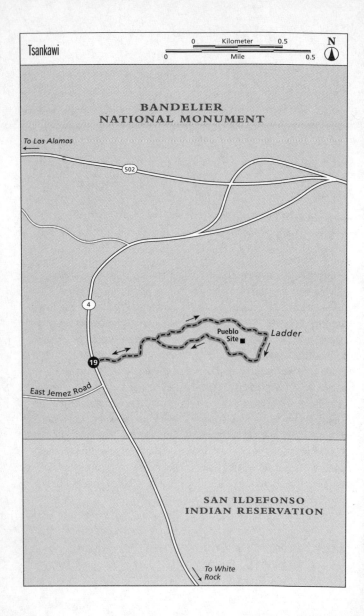

Tsankawi

0   Kilometer   0.5
0   Mile   0.5

N

BANDELIER
NATIONAL MONUMENT

To Los Alamos

502

4

19

Pueblo
Site

Ladder

East Jemez Road

SAN ILDEFONSO
INDIAN RESERVATION

To White
Rock

Maps: USGS White Rock quadrangle; Park map available at the Frijoles Canyon Visitor Center and at a kiosk upon entering Tsankawi. Sky Terrain map to Santa Fe, Bandelier, and Los Alamos and National Geographic Trails Illustrated Map, Bandelier, both available at Travel Bug, 839 Paseo de Peralta, Santa Fe; (505) 992-0418; www.mapsof newmexico.com.

Trail contact: Bandelier National Monument Headquarters, 15 Entrance Rd., Los Alamos, NM 87544; (505) 672-3861, ext. 517; www.nps.gov/band

Special considerations: This trail includes narrow passageways and ladders. It is exposed in summer heat. Remember, do not disturb or remove any artifacts, pottery, rocks, plants, or wildlife. Do not deface cliffs or caves. Stay on the trail, as the underlying rock is extremely susceptible to erosion.

Finding the trailhead: From Santa Fe take US 285/84 north to Pojoaque. At Pojoaque take NM 502 west for approximately 12 miles to the junction with NM 4, following signs to Los Alamos. Take NM 4 (south), following signs for Bandelier National Monument and White Rock. In 0.7 mile you will see the long, narrow parking lot for Tsankawi on the left, immediately before the first traffic light. The trailhead is located through the gate and downhill a short distance. GPS: N35 51.36' / W106 13.28'

The Hike

Beyond the information kiosk the trail heads uphill. Very soon you will ascend a ladder to reach a small ledge, and the trail continues east. In a short distance you have the option to either walk left on a well-worn, narrow footpath that takes you to the mesa top (the same trail that the ancient people who lived here used centuries ago), or you may walk a short distance to the right and ascend the ladder to the mesa top.

From the mesa top you will see the Jemez Mountains to your left (west). Straight ahead are the Sangre de Cristo Mountains and the Rio Grande Valley.

As you continue you will walk through the central plaza of the village. Near the end of the mesa you will see a low wall that may have held a small reservoir. Beyond the wall the trail descends a 12-foot ladder and continues on narrow paths.

You may wish to return the way you came, but to complete the loop, climb down the ladder at the cliff's edge, and follow the trail as it continues to the right as you face away from the ladder. As you walk, you will see your first cavate. You are asked to visit only those cavates closest to the trail to avoid creating unnecessary trails in the soft rock.

Keep on the lookout for petroglyphs as you walk on ancient trails on the lower ledge, and return to the rock platform near the beginning of the trail. From the intersection of the loop, it is a short distance back to the trailhead.

20 Cerro Grande

Cerro Grande (Big Mountain) Trail, located in the western part of Bandelier National Monument, takes you to the highest point in the park at 10,199 feet. The mountain forms part of the rim of the Valles Caldera, a crater formed after a volcanic eruption 1.2 million years ago. From the summit you have a panoramic view of the Sangre de Cristo and Sandia Mountains, and a bird's-eye view of the Valles Caldera. The diverse and serene landscape makes you forget the substantial elevation gain.

Distance: 4.6 miles out and back
Ascent: 1,300 feet
Hiking time: About 3 hours
Difficulty: Strenuous
Trail surface: Dirt
Best season: Late spring, summer, fall
Other trail users: Runners
Canine compatibility: Dogs not permitted
Fees and permits: None
Schedule: Trail open daily, year-round, from dawn to dusk
Maps: Park map available at the Bandelier National Monument visitor center in Frijoles Canyon. Printable maps available at www.nps.gov/band and www.american southwest.net/new_mexico/ban delier/national_monument.html. Bandelier National Monument Map by National Geographic/ Trails Illustrated. Sky Terrain map to Santa Fe, Bandelier, and Los Alamos available at Travel Bug, 839 Paseo de Peralta, Santa Fe; (505) 992-0418; www.mapsof newmexico.com
Trail contact: Bandelier National Monument Headquarters, 15 Entrance Rd., Los Alamos, NM 87544; (505) 672-3861, ext. 517; www.nps.gov/band
Special considerations: Stay away from the summit in storms.

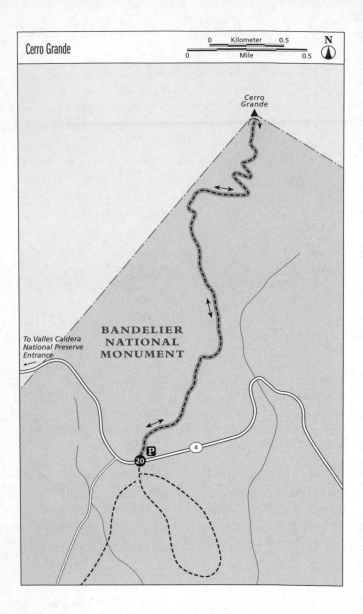

Cerro Grande

Cerro
Grande

N

To Valles Caldera
National Preserve
Entrance

BANDELIER
NATIONAL
MONUMENT

P

20

4

0   Kilometer   0.5

0   Mile   0.5

Finding the trailhead: From Santa Fe drive north on US 84/285. In Pojoaque take NM 502 west for approximately 12 miles to the junction with NM 4, following signs to Los Alamos. Take NM 4 south for 12.1 miles, passing the main entrance to Bandelier National Monument. Continue on NM 4, passing the Ponderosa Campground on your left and the junction with NM 501 (observe the old Los Alamos security gate) on your right. From here the trailhead parking area is about 5.9 miles farther uphill into the Jemez Mountains. It is well marked. GPS: N35 50.52' / W106 25.20'

The Hike

As you hike, be aware of the yellow diamonds on trees marking the way. The trail sets off in a rather open forest of mature ponderosa and aspen, and may have beautifully green underbrush after an early and intense monsoon season.

The trail then heads up a very gentle slope, coming alongside a fenced-off area (elk enclosure) beside a large meadow. As you continue around the mountainside, the highway becomes visible.

At about 1.4 miles the trail comes to a saddle and a grassy meadow. It then takes you through the meadow into a lightly wooded area and proceeds up a series of switchbacks. The summit is a short distance away, and there you will find a large cairn to which you can add your own rock, marking your accomplishment.

Look around for panoramic views of a large section of the Valles Caldera to the west. To the east and south you can see much of Bandelier, the Rio Grande Valley, and the Sangre de Cristo and Sandia mountain ranges.

Retrace your steps, following the yellow diamonds and directional arrows back to the trailhead.

Valles Caldera National Preserve

The Valles Caldera was formed over six million years ago by a series of volcanic eruptions that ejected a volume of materials five hundred times greater than the May 1980 eruption of Mount Saint Helens. The volcanic ash covered more than 100 square miles and created the canyon and mesa landscape of the Pajarito Plateau, including landforms in nearby Bandelier National Monument and around the city of Los Alamos. Redondo Peak, at 11,254 feet, is a dominant feature of this collapsed crater, which is also studded with many smaller volcanic domes throughout its acreage.

This 89,000-acre preserve has a long history of ownership. It was once held by the Baca family, part of New Mexico's history since the 1600s, and became part of the National Park Service on Sept. 30, 2015. Although substantial access to many hiking trails in the heart of the caldera was in effect at the time this guide was researched, the National Park Service's future plans had not yet been made public, and accessibility may change in the near future. Visit www.vallescaldera.gov or call toll-free (866) 382-5537.

21 Cerro La Jara Loop

This easy walk around the beautiful Cerro La Jara volcanic dome traverses open, grassy meadows and provides a 360-degree view of the Valle Grande. Although many hikes take you deeper into the caldera and were open when this guide was researched, you can experience the beauty of the Valles Caldera on this short, easy hike. It is also very well suited for children. The volcanic dome of La Jara resembles a small island in a sea of wildflowers when visited during an early and intense monsoon season.

Distance: 1.6-mile loop
Ascent: 152 feet
Hiking time: About 1 hour
Difficulty: Easy
Trail surface: This dirt and grass path is not well-defined in many places. Numbered signposts indicate the direction to hike around the mountain.
Best season: Spring, summer (can be wet), fall. Cross-country skiing in winter.
Other trail users: Skiers
Canine compatibility: Dogs are not permitted in the Valles Caldera backcountry or on trails, although service animals are allowed in the preserve. Pets may accompany you in some designated areas (must be caged, crated, or leashed) but are not allowed in many areas. Equestrian trails are limited (check the website); fishing is permitted.
Fees and permits: An entry fee is charged; all federally issued park passes are accepted.
Schedule: The Preserve is open daily year-round. Summer (May 15 to Oct 1) 8 a.m. to 6 p.m.; winter (Oct 1 to May 14) 9 a.m. to 5 p.m.
Maps: USGS Bland NM. Preserve map available at the visitor center in the staging area. Valles Caldera Map High Desert Field Guides, available at Travel Bug, 839 Paseo de Peralta, Santa Fe; (505) 992-0418; www.mapsof newmexico.com; online at www .nps.gov/vall/planyourvisit/maps .htm.

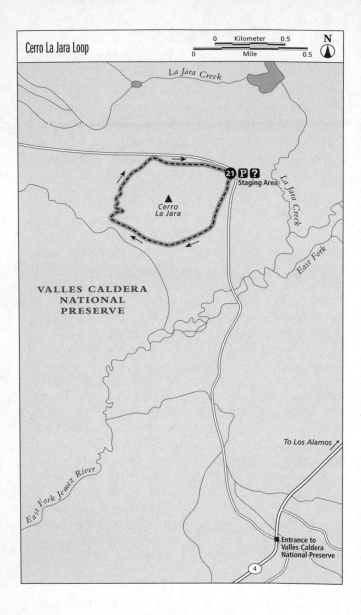

Cerro La Jara Loop

0   Kilometer   0.5
0   Mile   0.5

N

La Jara Creek

Cerro
La Jara

21 P ?
Staging Area

La Jara Creek

East Fork

VALLES CALDERA
NATIONAL
PRESERVE

To Los Alamos

East Fork Jemez River

Entrance to
Valles Caldera
National Preserve

4

Trail contacts: Valles Caldera National Preserve, PO Box 359, Jemez Springs, NM 87025, (575) 829-4100, www.vallescalera.gov;

Visitor center: (505) 670-1612; info@vallescaldera.gov
Special considerations: Take along the laminated trail guide available at the visitor center.

Finding the trailhead: From Santa Fe drive north on US 84/285. In Pojoaque take NM 502 west for approximately 12 miles, following signs for Los Alamos. This route will afford you great views of the Pajarito Plateau, Black Mesa, and an opportunity to visit San Ildefonso Indian Reservation on your right before you drive over the Rio Grande. At about 12 miles take NM 4 west, following the signs for White Rock and Bandelier National Monument. At 1.4 miles (the first light), go right onto East Jemez Road, the truck route to Los Alamos. When you enter the city, turn left at the first light, following the signs for Valles Caldera and NM 501. Almost immediately you will drive through a security check for the Los Alamos National Laboratory, at which you need only show picture identification. Proceed for 4.6 miles. The road will end at the junction with NM 4. Turn right and drive for approximately 10.4 miles, where you will see the entrance for the Valles Caldera National Preserve. Proceed on the dirt road to the staging area (approximately 4 miles). Start your hike at the trailhead adjacent to the visitor center, where you will check in before you begin. GPS: N35 51.14' / W106 29.59'

The Hike

The hike starts on a marked path just south of the staging area. After hiking a short while, a La Jara sign directs you to continue right.

At about 0.6 mile, you will see a sign for "Missing Cabin." Look right to see post #3 in the distance. This is your next marker. Be careful to follow the numbered posts to avoid veering off onto a lightly used road that leads to the left and away from the trail.

Continue to follow the numbered signposts, passing a picnic table amid a few large boulders on your right. Complete the loop at the staging area where you began.

Los Alamos

The hiking trails around Los Alamos are more remote and receive less use than the trails closer to Santa Fe. On your way to the trailhead, a trip to this once secret city is highly encouraged.

The Bradbury Science Museum, located on Central Avenue, offers a detailed history of the Los Alamos National Laboratory and its ongoing science and research. In the History Gallery be sure not to miss the sixteen-minute film summarizing the story of the Manhattan Project and the history of Los Alamos from 1942 to 1945.

A short drive west on Central Avenue brings you to the Fuller Lodge complex. This beautiful log structure was built in 1928 and was the center of activity for the Ranch School, which was later to become the heart of the Manhattan Project and the city of Los Alamos. In an adjacent building, also a historical Ranch School structure, you will find the Los Alamos Historical Museum and Book Shop. In addition to offering a wonderful miniview of the geological history of the Pajarito Plateau, and exhibits and memorabilia from the early days of Los Alamos, the museum also offers guided walking tours of the city and self-guiding pamphlets. Don't miss a stroll down Bathtub Row, where Robert Oppenheimer and Hans Bethe, among other early scientists, lived.

For more information on the historical museum visit www.losalamoshistory.org.

On December 19, 2014, President Obama signed authorization for the creation of the Manhattan Project National Historical Park. The park will include the US Department of Energy's most significant Manhattan Project properties, of which Los Alamos is but one. The details will be many years in the making, and you may keep abreast of progress at www.energy.gov.

As in Santa Fe, Los Alamos has developed a network of urban trails. The foothills, canyons, and mesas in and around Los Alamos are linked by a 58-mile network of trails. The visitor center/chamber of commerce in the city center has maps and information, or you can visit www.losalamosnm.us/parks.

22 Guaje Canyon Trail

This hike begins north of Los Alamos at the Pajarito Mountain Ski Area and gives an easy introduction to the gentle and inviting Jemez Mountains. The beautiful meadow, Cañada Bonita, lies directly in your path, and you skirt it for breathtaking views of the Valles Caldera. The forest immediately surrounding the trail was, for the most part, spared the devastation of both the Cerro Grande fire of 2000 and the Las Conchas fire of 2011.

Distance: 5.6 miles out and back
Ascent: 430 feet
Hiking time: About 3 hours
Difficulty: Moderate
Trail surface: Forested trail
Best season: Fall, late spring, summer (Nordic and cross-country skiing in winter)
Other trail users: Mountain bikers
Canine compatibility: Leashed dogs permitted. Please pick up after your dog.
Fees and permits: None
Schedule: Year-round
Maps: USGS Valle Toledo NM. USDA Forest Service map to Santa Fe National Forest. Sky Terrain map to Santa Fe, Bandelier, and Los Alamos available at Travel Bug, 829 Paseo de Peralta, Santa Fe; (505) 992-0418; mapsofnewmexico.com
Trail contact: Santa Fe National Forest; 1710 N. Riverside Dr., Espanola, NM 87532; (505) 438-5300. Espanola Ranger District; (505) 753-7331; www.fs .usda.gov/santafe
Special considerations: The trail is susceptible to tree fall during strong winds such as those associated with afternoon thunderstorms in summer.

Finding the trailhead: From Santa Fe take US 285/84 north to Pojoaque. At Pojoaque take NM 502 west for approximately 12 miles to the junction with NM 4, following signs for Los Alamos. Take NM

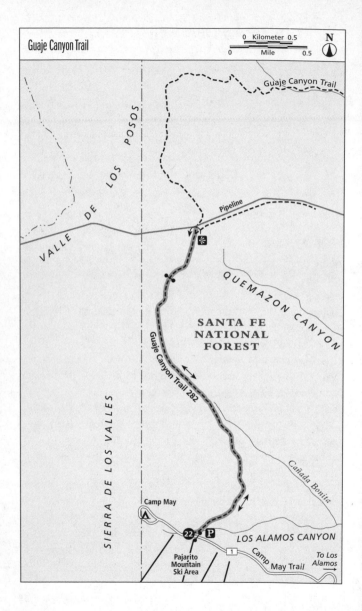

4 west, following the signs for White Rock and Bandelier National Monument. At 1.4 miles (the first light), go right on East Jemez Road, the truck route to Los Alamos. When you enter the city, turn left at the first light and the signs for Valles Caldera and NM 501. Almost immediately you will drive through a security check for the Los Alamos National Laboratory and will be asked to show picture identification. Proceed straight, past the Los Alamos National Laboratory on your left, for 1.4 miles. Turn right onto Camp May Trail and drive for just 0.3 mile, turning left onto Ski Hill Rd. Drive another 5.6 miles to the parking lot for Pajarito Mountain Ski Area. Park at the far end of the parking lot and walk downhill, where you will take the first trail off to the right. There is a forest service bulletin board at the beginning of Guaje Trail 282. GPS: N35 53.45' / W106 23.36'

The Hike

Guaje Trail 282 heads northeast on an old forest road, and almost immediately you must go around or under a gate. Stay on the main trail (avoiding the cross-country ski trail on the left) as it passes through a beautiful mixed conifer forest and ascends slightly for about 1 mile.

You will then come to a large meadow called Cañada Bonita (pretty watercourse), which is a US Forest Service Research Natural Area, protected because of its unique montane grassland. The trail skirts the meadow (filled with wildflowers in July) for about 1 mile, turns north, and begins an ascent, retreating back into the shade of aspens. At a forest service sign (about 2.6 miles), walk through an open gate. Continue walking straight ahead, through a small clearing in the woods, and in a short distance you will see a marker for a pipeline and also a sign denoting Guaje Canyon Trail. Walk a short distance to your left to an overlook providing vistas into Valle San Antonio, part of the larger Valles Caldera.

Return to the trailhead by retracing your route.

23 Bayo Benches Loop

The Los Alamos County Trail Network offers hikers, runners, mountain bikers, and equestrians more than 75 miles of trail to explore. This particular hike explores a typical Los Alamos canyon that includes a fantastic view. The trail takes you on hundred-year-old homestead roads (created to transport people and goods from the bottom of Bayo Canyon to the mesa tops in Los Alamos) throughout the hike.

Distance: 4.5-mile lollipop
Ascent: 674 feet
Hiking time: About 2.5 hours
Difficulty: Moderate
Trail surface: Dirt, rock, forested trail
Best season: Spring, summer, fall
Other trail users: Mountain bikers, equestrians, joggers
Canine compatibility: All dogs must be leashed within 100 yards of trailhead and under voice and sight control at all times.
Fees and permits: None
Schedule: Year-round
Maps: Available at Los Alamos County Parks Division, 101 Camino Entrada, Building 5, Los Alamos; (505) 662-8159. Los Alamos Chamber of Commerce and Visitor Center, 109 Central Park Square, Los Alamos; (505) 662-8105; download at www .losalamosnm.us/parks/trails
Trail contacts: Los Alamos County Parks Division, 101 Camino Entrada, Building 5, Los Alamos; www.losalamos.us/ parks; (505) 662-8159. Los Alamos County Open Space and Trails,101 Camino Entrada, Bldg. 5, Los Alamos, NM 87544; www .losalamosnm.us/parks/trails; (505) 663-1776
Special considerations: Watch children at the overlook. Several unmarked trails intersect with this one. Do not worry, as they generally come back to the main trail, and it is easy to determine your location in the canyon throughout the hike.

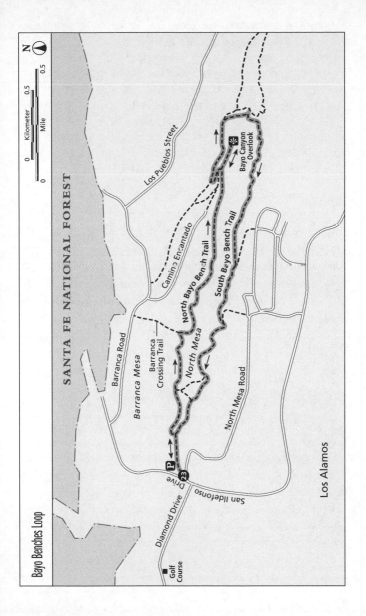

Bayo Benches Loop

SANTA FE NATIONAL FOREST

Los Pueblos Street

Bayo Canyon Overlook

Camino Encantado

North Bayo Bench Trail

South Bayo Bench Trail

North Mesa

Barranca Mesa

Barranca Crossing Trail

Barranca Road

North Mesa Road

Los Alamos

Diamond Drive

San Ildefonso Drive

23

P

Golf Course

N

0   0.5
Kilometer
0   0.5
Mile

Finding the trailhead: From downtown Los Alamos at the intersection of 15th Street and Central Avenue, head west (toward the Jemez Mountains) on Central Avenue. In 0.8 mile turn right onto Diamond Drive. Set your odometer. You will pass Los Alamos High School on your right; stay on Diamond Drive and eventually pass the golf course, which is on both sides of the road. At about 2.4 miles you will come to the San Ildefonso roundabout. Circle halfway through the roundabout and briefly head uphill on North Mesa Road. The trailhead is about 100 feet from the roundabout on the left, and there is parking for about six vehicles. GPS: N35 53.59' / W106 17.53'

The Hike

After parking your car, head downhill and turn right after the informational kiosk. Walk east across an open space and then take the left fork, North Bayo Bench Trail. Follow this trail as it heads east on a narrow bench, about 50 feet below the mesa top. The rather open ponderosa pine forest offers some shade on hot summer days.

After about 1.6 miles a trail to the right takes you to the Bayo Canyon overlook. From here there are great vistas of both the Jemez and Sangre de Cristo mountain ranges.

Return to the main trail, which takes a sharp right and descends down the mesa on an old homestead road with ruts worn by wagons that used to climb to homesteads on the mesa top.

When you reach the bottom, veer to the right on a narrower path, crossing the canyon bottom and continuing to the right on the south side of the canyon. You will slowly ascend the canyon. About 4 miles into the hike, the trail splits. Hike left, uphill, and walk the remaining 0.5 mile back to the trailhead.

Pecos Wilderness

The 222,673-acre Pecos Wilderness, most of which is located within the Santa Fe National Forest, lies 35 miles northeast of Santa Fe. Within its boundaries are many peaks over 13,000 feet, mountain lakes, and more than 50 miles of pristine streams. This area is heavily used by hikers and horses; therefore, consider getting out early on weekends, especially if you are planning to locate a campsite in one of the many very accessible and well-maintained campgrounds. Motorized equipment and mechanized transportation, including mountain bikes, are prohibited in the Pecos Wilderness.

We have only one hike in this beautiful wilderness area that we deemed "best" and "easy." However, with a little investigation you can find others that will take you deeper into the wilderness.

It is well worth your time to visit the Pecos National Historical Park in the village of Pecos (take the second exit for Pecos; exit 307, coming from Santa Fe, and follow the signs). The wonderful museum offers a compact and complete history of New Mexico, a bookstore, and an informative film depicting the history of the ancient Pecos Pueblo. There is also a 1.25-mile self-guided tour that winds through the ruins of the pueblo, established during the fourteenth century. The original mission church was destroyed during the

Pueblo Revolt of 1620, but was rebuilt in 1717; its ruins are a prominent feature of the monument.

The Civil War Battle of Glorieta Pass (March 26–28, 1862) is an important part of New Mexico history, and the national monument provides information on the battle, which occurred close by. Access to actual sites is limited but guided tours are often available.

For more information contact Pecos National Historical Park, PO Box 418, Pecos, NM 87552-0418; (505) 757-7241; www.nps.gov/peco. Leashed dogs are permitted. Hours are from 8 a.m. to 4:30 p.m. daily from Labor Day to Memorial Day, and 8 a.m. to 6 p.m. from Memorial Day to Labor Day. An entrance fee is charged; parks passes are accepted.

24 Cave Creek Trail

This hike on trail 288 takes you to a set of caves along picturesque Cave Creek in the Pecos Wilderness. You'll walk through lush forests of Douglas fir, aspen, and blue spruce. Wildflowers are varied and plentiful. It is appropriate as a family hike and a wonderful introduction to the Pecos Wilderness.

Distance: 4.1 miles out and back

Ascent: 500 feet

Hiking time: About 2 hours

Difficulty: Moderate

Trail surface: Dirt, rock

Best season: Spring, summer, fall

Other trail users: This trail receives heavy use by horses. Fishing is permitted; mountain bikes are not permitted.

Canine compatibility: Leashed dogs permitted

Fees and permits: A parking fee is charged.

Schedule: Year-round

Maps: USGS Cowles NM; USDA Forest Service. Santa Fe National Forest Pecos Wilderness Map.

Trail contacts: Santa Fe National Forest Pecos/Las Vegas Ranger District, PO Drawer 429, Pecos, NM 87552; (505) 757-6121; www.us.fs.usda.gov

Special considerations: The crossing of Panchuela Creek can be precarious during spring and early summer runoff and during monsoon season.

Finding the trailhead: From Santa Fe take I-25 toward Las Vegas. Take exit 299 (first Pecos exit) for NM 50, Glorieta and Pecos. Follow NM 50 to the town of Pecos and the intersection with NM 63. Turn left onto NM 63 and drive 20 miles to Cowles. In Cowles turn left, over the bridge crossing the Pecos River and take the first right onto single-lane, paved FR 305 to Panchuela picnic area (a former campground).

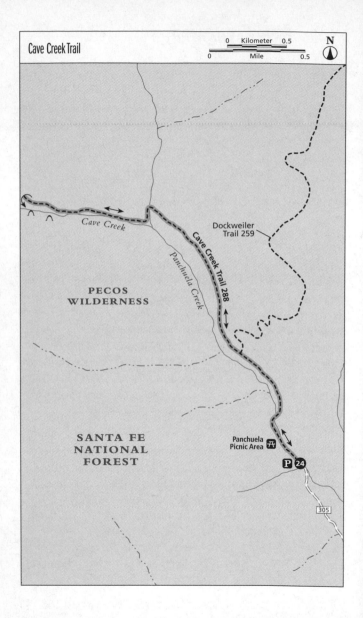

Cave Creek Trail

0   Kilometer   0.5

0   Mile   0.5

N

Cave Creek

Dockweiler
Trail 259

Cave Creek Trail 288

Panchuela Creek

PECOS
WILDERNESS

SANTA FE
NATIONAL
FOREST

Panchuela
Picnic Area

P 24

305

The large parking lot is the location of the trailhead. GPS: N35 49.54' /
W105 39.53'

The Hike

The trail begins at the parking lot bulletin board. Walk to
the left, through the picnic area and over the bridge crossing
Panchuela Creek, continuing a gradual climb upstream to
the left on Cave Creek Trail 288. The large, old Douglas fir
along the trail are impressive. As you hike the trail parallels
the creek, rises above it, and at about 0.8 mile comes to a
junction with Dockweiler Trail 259, which forks to the right.
Stay left (west) on Cave Creek Trail as it winds through the
valley. You may see people hiking out after a successful day
of fishing along this route.

At about 1.5 miles you will reach the confluence of Panchuela and Cave Creeks. Follow the trail to the left (west)
over several logs, which make a somewhat risky bridge. This
is a beautiful spot to stop, rest, and examine the lush riparian
vegetation.

The first set of caves lies about 0.4 mile up the trail on
your left (south). A small cairn and well-worn path mark
the location. The caves were formed by water seeping into
fractures in the limestone, and they are surprisingly deep. To
find the second set of caves, look for a clearing and another
path to the creek less than 0.1 mile farther on the trail. You
can cross the creek to examine the caves; however, the rocks
are very slippery, and there are deep dropoffs inside the caves,
so it is not entirely safe to enter them.

After a rest, retrace your steps back to the trailhead.

About the Authors

Linda Black Regnier divides her time between New Mexico (where she was raised) and Montana. She is an advocate for environmental and animal rights issues. Hope Di Paolo is pursuing a degree at Colgate University. They, along with husband and grandfather Jim, were grateful for an unexpected and wonderful summer together in New Mexico while writing this book. They urge those who read and use it to become involved in the work of preserving wilderness areas wherever they may be.

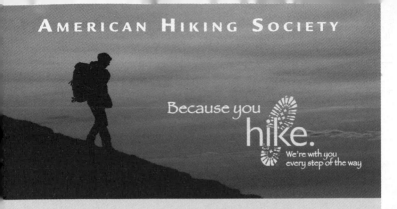